Ideas That WORK

Ideas That WORK

10 of Today's
Most Exciting and Profitable
Self-Employment Opportunities

Susan Elliott

Live Oak Publications
Boulder, Colorado

Library of Congress Cataloging in Publication Data

Elliott, Susan, 1950-
Ideas That Work.

1. Self-employed. 2. New business enterprises.
I. Title.
HD8036.E45 1985 658'.041 84-21860
ISBN O-911781-02-1

ISBN: 0-911781-02-1

Library of Congress Catalog Card Number: 84-21860

Published by Live Oak Publications
        6003 N. 51st Street
        P.O. Box 2193
        Boulder, CO 80306
        (303) 530-1087

Distributed by Liberty Publishing Company, Inc.
        50 Scott Adam Rd.
        Cockeysville, MD 21030
        (301) 667-6680

Contents

Chapter 1
Choosing Independence
Through Self-Employment

"We have on our hands an entrepreneurial boom the like of which we have not seen in a century. The most important economic event of the last few years, in fact, is the emergence of this entrepreneurial trend."

— Professor Peter Drucker
quoted in *U.S. News and World Report*

"This can*not* happen to me!" was Coralee Kerns' stunned reaction to her doctor's pronouncement that she, a 40-year-old divorced mother of two teenagers, would never be able to work again. Lupus, he told her, was a serious, debilitating illness; leading a normal life, holding down a nine-to-five job, was something a victim of the disease couldn't expect to do. There would be repeated stays in the hospital, days when merely getting out of bed would be too painful, too exhausting.

Black as her circumstances seemed at the time, today Coralee believes the diagnosis of her illness was one of the "marvelous things that happened to me that changed my life." Looking back, the turning point seemed to have come with her decision to start her own business, to find something interesting and challenging that could be operated from her own home.

As Coralee was shortly to find out, she was far from alone in thinking that self-employment in a service business had become an attractive, feasible option. According to the Bureau of Labor Statistics, the number of nonagricultural, nonincorporated self-employed workers rose 38 percent in the last ten years, reaching 7.58 million. More than half a million new businesses are now created annually.

Not only has there been a dramatic change in the *quantity* of the self-employed — there have been equally dramatic changes in the *quality* of self-employment. Generally speaking, the self-employed today are more prosperous than in the past, although they are younger now and work fewer hours per week. A surprisingly large number of the self-employed today are women. Consider the following:

- The earnings of people self-employed in incorporated businesses now far outstrip the pay of salary and wage earners.

- People are becoming self-employed at a younger age now. Ten years ago, about 60 percent of the self-employed were over 45; today, the ratio between those over 45 and younger workers (16 to 44) has shifted to roughly fifty-fifty.

- Today's entrepreneur works fewer hours than in the past. The average number of hours worked by the self-employed has dropped from 47 to about 42 a week.

- In the last ten years, the number of self-employed women increased at a rate more than five times that of men. Credit and lending laws which require equal treatment and give women greater access to credit are one factor contributing to this trend.

Why are increasing numbers of Americans opting for self-employment? For one thing, our value sytems have changed. Two generations of affluence have bred into us the conviction that we can and should like what we do for a living. For many of us, money and security have become less important than independence, control, and self-expression. Apart from the philosophical motivations, there are the hard practicalities confronting growing segments of our population: single parents and working mothers, for instance, must support their families while remaining available to them; senior citizens, forced from the job market by early retirement, are often unable to subsist on their pensions. Then there are those who, like Coralee, simply can't hold down nine-to-five jobs outside the home. Self-employment offers workable, profitable alternatives to each of these groups. As inflation continues to reduce buying power, as rising divorce rates create more single-parent families, and as our over-65 population continues to grow, greater numbers of Americans will choose self-employment.

Growth in Service Opportunities

As real as the above reasons are, they may be dwarfed in importance by another influence on self-employment — the unprecedented demand for services.

Economists frequently speak of the shift from an industrial economy to a services economy which is taking place. About 70 percent of all employees now work in a service; among the self-employed, the figure is 78 percent. Why the rising demand for services? Part of the answer has to do with today's increasingly hectic and complex lifestyle. As the frustrations and complexities of dealing with day-to-day life increase, more and more people turn to creative means of self-expression and personal growth out of self-defense. A heightened awareness of the value of time has resulted. By spending money on time-saving services, consumers can exert control and spend increased time at more rewarding activities.

Another reason for the growth in services has to do with the increasing numbers of women in the workplace. As more women join the workforce, more services are needed to manage the tasks traditionally reserved for homemakers. Child-care services and home cleaning services, for example, are both growing rapidly.

Changes in our economy, with new industries emerging and others declining, have also contributed to the growth in services. With small firms intensely competing in rapidly growing industries there is a tendency to rely on freelance service businesses and out-side consultants rather than tying up scarce capital in salaries, training and benefits. To a degree, the growth of small business is self-perpetuating: As new small businesses come into existence, they create new demand for the types of services best provided by other small businesses.

Finally, technological advances have made certain kinds of services — word processing, photocopying and offset printing, for example — essentially one-person operations, opening new doors for the entrepreneur with only minimal capital.

A Few Examples

Today, Coralee Kern's Chicago-based "Maid to Order" is one of the largest service businesses in the country. With more than 400 employees, she provides maids, butlers and bartenders for about 1,000 parties a year in addition to the cleaning services she offers. As head of the National Association for the Cottage Industry, Cor-alee also promotes networking among home-based businesses. She is in great demand as a guest speaker at junior colleges and adult education facilities, where she conducts workshops for prospective entrepreneurs. Quite a striking list of accomplishments, all things considered. How did she do it?

"I assessed my skills," Coralee says. "I knew, absolutely without question, that my best skill was my ability to talk on the phone. I knew that I could do any kind of business there was that could be done on the phone." She and her children brainstormed and together came up with three ideas for businesses Coralee could run from their apartment. "Stop right there!" Coralee's mother cried when they told her about their idea for a maid service. "I've got the perfect name for you: "Maid To Order: Your Blue Chip Mail Service." It was a great name, Coralee agreed. A maid service it would be.

Before launching the business, however, she first set out to determine just how much demand existed for a new maid service. "We did our homework. I sent my son down to sit outside high-rise apartment buildings at seven o'clock in the morning. I gave him a sheet of paper and told him to write down who the people were who were going into the buildings and how many he thought were maids. Then I called the building manager to find out how large the building was, how many square feet, how many kitchens, how many bathrooms."

Once Coralee had determined that there was unmet demand for cleaning services, her next step was to find ways to introduce herself to her prospective customers. "I wanted to give people a bath in our name. We sent out announcements on blue paper, handwritten with blue ink, using blue commemorative stamps. Maids wore white in Chicago. We decided our maids would never wear white. Instead, we dressed our maids in gold, and used the slogan "Our maids are as good as gold." We also did a promotion for years that said "Our maids will leave your apartment fresh as a daisy. We sent daisies to 73 building managers and, at the same time, we sent the same message to all the tenants by direct mail. We ordered hundreds of thousands of magnetic daisies — no message, just daisies — and we sent them to doormen, receiving room men and building managers and asked them to give them away by the handful."

Did it work?

"People still talk about it."

Although Maid To Order has long since expanded to two offices, Coralee continues to work out of her home. At first she wasn't anxious to tell people that, however: "See, twelve years ago when I started, I lied to everybody. Back then I felt you had to have a downtown office, so I rented a fake address downtown, made them think I was a chief honcho down on South Madison Avenue. Now you don't need to conceal the fact that you're a home-based business. In fact, now on the outsides of our envelopes we have printed, 'We are a cottage industry.' "

Coralee's success provides an inspiring example of overcoming a handicap (in this case a debilitating illness) through perseverance and determination. She is modest about her achievements. "When I went into business, all I wanted to do was keep body and soul together and not have to collect Social Security. I've had a lot of nice things happen to me."

Al Sutherland, Home Sitters Service

In 1971, Al Sutherland was a 66-year-old, newly retired insurance man, chafing at the prospect of spending the rest of his life "sitting on a shelf, waiting for the old man with the scythe." He was still healthy, alert, capable — and he wanted to *do* something with his energy and experience. What's more, he knew other retired men and women shared his feelings. He understood the two major problems confronting the retired: inflation and boredom. "There are a lot of things retired people can't do because of income. Unless people keep actively involved in life and living, they deteriorate both mentally and physically."

Al perceived a mutual need, as well as a mutual opportunity. He would establish a home sitting service — a service which would provide people to look after property, pets and plants while homeowners are away — and which would employ only retired people. The plan proved to be a boon to both his employees and his customers. The sitters love it, he says. "It brings them back to being useful human beings again. They feel needed and appreciated." And the customers? "They're delighted. All they need to do is pack their bags, call us and go."

Free publicity gave Al's idea momentum when a local newspaper, charmed by the idea of "an old fellow starting something after he retired," ran a feature article about Home Sitters in a Sunday supplement. Within two weeks he had thirty-five calls from people offering to sit. Now, twelve years later, Al's idea has caught on to such an extent that he and his son, who joined the firm four years ago, now market their business know-how to entrepreneurs in other cities. There are currently more than forty independently owned and operated divisions of Home Sitters Services in cities from coast to coast, with new ones being opened every month.

Connie Cox, Home Management Systems

At 35, Connie Cox had it all: marvelous husband, charming three-year-old son, beautiful turn-of-the-century home, prestigious career as a probate lawyer. She remembers now how baffling and frustrating it was to be in such an enviable position and yet feel that something important was missing. She has this to say about her law practice: "It was okay, but it never touched my soul. It never made me feel as though I was making that contribution I wanted to make or that I was growing in the way that I wanted." With her considerable training — she had received her degree in history from UC Berkeley, along with a masters in education from Stanford University — she knew she could do any number of things. But what? She enjoyed teaching, but two years in public schools had showed her that "recalcitrant eighth-graders" aren't the most amenable students. She needed time to regroup. At last, she decided to quit practicing law and take a year off to reconsider her priorities.

After a few short weeks at home, Connie realized that if and when she discovered what it was she wanted to do, she would need time to do it — time unencumbered by driving carpools and running errands, finding swim trunks and making school lunches. Feeling herself bogged down in the mechanics of keeping everybody fed and dressed, she thought to herself, "This is crazy. Running a house is not a full-time career." She took a look at the way her days were occupied and decided she had a real problem with organization. I did not like it," she says, describing the chaos that often reigned. "First of all, it was wasteful. Secondly, there wasn't a lot of quality going on. It was my one chance to be a mom and I was muffing it away. Also, I wasn't doing a very good job of being a wife. What happened was that I [had] scheduled myself to have no personal time."

In the process of solving her own organization problems, Connie stumbled across the concept for a home-based business, something that would use her skills while providing that longed-for sense of fulfillment. She would conduct home management seminars in which she would teach other people how to organize their routines and fulfill their obligations in such a way as to carve out big chunks of time for pursuing whatever soul-nurturing activities *they* liked. The seminars wouldn't be just for career women but for anyone who wanted to create time to have lunch with friends, take tennis lessons — or simply have more time for reading. Connie saw that what was needed was a set of systems for handling time-consuming tasks like shopping, meal planning, home maintenance, and financial record keeping. She also recognized that even in households where both partners took part in making things run, somebody had to be in charge. "Somebody has to be on top of the systems."

It wasn't hard at all to get twenty friends together for the pilot seminar, and the enthusiastic participants provided Connie with helpful feedback as well as referrals. The day-long seminar, which is held in hotel conference rooms and includes lunch, covers such topics as record keeping, storage and space management, setting up a home office, as well as meal planning and delegating household tasks. The response, says Connie, has been overwhelming, with over 400 people attending seminars during the first year alone.

Although Home Management Systems began turning a profit within the first year, Connie feels that an even greater reward than income has been the personal satisfaction she's gained. "I have never met so many wonderful people in such a short period of time," she says. "There are 400 people who've taken that class, and I could probably be friends with 395 of them." Asked if she felt she was finally achieving the goals she had set for herself, if she had, at last, found something that "touched her soul," she replied, "You bet. I mean I love to teach seminars. I might pay someone else to do the office work, but it will be a long time before I have someone else do the seminars. That's the turn-on."

You Can Do It Too

Perhaps you can see yourself in one of these examples. Maybe you'd like to lift the ceiling from your income and write your own job description. It could be more freedom or flexibility you crave — or maybe you've just been to one too many office Christmas parties. Regardless of your reasons for considering self-employment, you should realize that, although it may not be easy, becoming your own boss is an attainable goal.

Chapter 2
Keys to Success

This chapter is about minimizing risk and maximizing your chances of succeeding in your own small business. A certain amount of trial and error fumbling is probably unavoidable in any new venture; the trick is to realize this and make every effort to limit the downside risk and concentrate your resources on your idea's upside potential.

Key Number 1 — Choose the Right Business

What is the right business for you? It can be a difficult question, and it's possible to get so wrapped up in trying to find the perfect business that you never get around to actually taking the plunge. Here are some things to consider.

First of all, take a good look at opportunities in services. As mentioned previously, the demand for services is growing at an unprecedented rate, and there are several advantages to starting this type of business:

- *Services are the easiest businesses to start.* Because they generally require less capital than other types of businesses, they also involve less risk.

- *Service businesses are often ideal businesses to operate from home.* There is no need for extensive inventory, so little storage space is usually required.

- *Some service businesses can be operated by a single person, and extra help can often be obtained on a contract-labor basis as needed.* This eliminates a tremendous amount of bookkeeping and paperwork, as well as expenses for Workman's Compensation, unemployment insurance, etc.

- *Extensive training, advanced degrees or other credentials are often unnecessary.* Your experience and practical knowledge may be more important to your success.

- *Service ventures can be extremely flexible.* By limiting or expanding your client list you can determine the amount of time you'll spend at your business. You also have the option of starting out slowly, working part time until your cash flow is established.

- *Service businesses respond well to the personal touch.* By taking a personal interest in your clients and their needs you can develop good will, repeat business and valuable word-of-mouth advertising.

What is a Service Business?

Each of the individuals profiled in chapter one are self-employed in a service business, as are all of the other people you'll meet in this book. Unlike businesses which deal with products, service businesses deal with intangibles, and a service exists only as it is performed. While services fill a variety of consumer needs, the basic commodity a service offers is time.

Enter a service field and you'll have the built-in advantage of being on top of a cultural trend. In addition to simply freeing up time for the consumer, services also respond to the needs of an economy in which speed is critical — we need everything "yesterday." In a culture characterized by an accelerating rate of change, services can only continue to grow in importance.

What Kind of Service Business?

Clearly there are some good reasons for choosing a service opportunity over, say, retailing or manufacturing, but what *kind* of a service opportunity? Each of the ten service opportunities covered in this book were chosen because they offer solid growth potential, and you may decide that one sounds right for you. Three criteria which might help you decide are 1) your skills, experience and interests, 2) any competitive advantages you may have, and 3) the market conditions where you live.

An important factor in the success of many new ventures is that their owners had a head start — they exploited skills and experience which they already possessed. Recall that Connie Cox had a masters degree in education. Her field experience in the war zone of junior high algebra made adult seminars seem like a snap.

Sometimes it's hard to be objective about your own skills and interests. The following exercise is a simple but powerful way to help overcome this obstacle. Take no more than ten minutes and very quickly make a list of things that you have done in your life which 1) were successful and 2) gave you a genuine sense of accomplishment. List as many of these activities as you can think of within the time limit.

Once you have your list go back over it and see what the common denominators are. Are the activities all "people" activities? Do they suggest creativity, or perhaps unexplored mechanical abilities? Whatever recurring themes you spot can be important clues to the types of self-employment you would thrive at.

Competitive advantages are another criteria. Try to think of ways that contacts and resources you have access to could help you in establishing your business. A relative in the real estate business, for example, might be able to refer a steady stream of clients to you if you were to begin a property management service. If you were to start a new word-processing service, your friend who works in a nearby office building might be able to ensure that her company's overflow work would be referred to you. Any advantages you can pinpoint that are unique to you can greatly increase your chances of success.

Perhaps most important of all are the market conditions where you live. Regardless of the type of business you're considering it would be foolhardy to invest your time and money before making sure that a market exists to support your business. What are the needs and opportunities in your community? Check the Yellow Pages to see if there are already others in the business you're planning. Even if there are services similar to what you are planning, it doesn't necessarily mean the field is glutted. You might have something unique to offer, or an especially appealing way of presenting your service.

Key Number 2 — Minimize Risk

It can be exhilerating to make the decision to strike out on your own and then come up with an idea that seems like a winner. Unfortunately too many people throw caution to the winds at this point, writing checks as if their success were already ensured and rationalizing the mounting bills as tax deductible expenses without even considering less expensive approaches to launching their business.

If you're smart you'll proceed slowly and cautiously in the beginning, carefully weighing alternatives and rationing whatever capital you have. Try to start your business on a part-time basis at first, keeping your job so you'll have a steady income to rely on. If you lack experience in the business you're interested in, by all means consider getting a job where you can learn the ins and outs and hidden pitfalls of that particular business before taking the plunge yourself.

To really minimize risk, you will need to do everything possible to keep your overhead expenses low. Remember that if you can save $1000 a year by cutting corners and keeping expenses down, the effect is about the same as increasing sales by $30,000 if your net profit is normally 3 percent. It is often far easier to cut costs than to increase sales by such large amounts. Buy only the supplies and tools you really need, consider leasing equipment rather than buying, and try the less expensive types of promotion in the beginning. It is true that you have to spend money to make money and inexpensive promotion methods may not work for your particular type of service, but at the least you will learn by trying them and you may be pleasantly surprised by the response.

Working From Home

One of the most effective ways to minimize overhead — and risk — is to turn your living space into an income-generating asset by working from your home or apartment. In his book *The Third Wave*, futurist Alvin Toffler has predicted that up to half of our future work force will spend at least part of their working lives working from home. And, as Coralee Kerns points out, if a home-based business ever was considered unprofessional, that attitude is rapidly changing. Today there often is no good reason not to make your home do double duty as an office. Here are just a few of the many advantages:

- A home business allows you to test an idea with a minimal investment. Not only do you not have to pay for expensive office space, you can also deduct a portion of your rent or mortgage payment from your annual taxable income. The same is also true for other household expenses such as phone and utility bills.

- Working at home means the end of:
  — rush hour commuting
  — usurious parking rates
  — fast food lunches
  — company politics

- You can arrange your working hours to suit your own needs and energy levels. If you want to put in twelve hours on a rainy day in order to spend the next sunny one on the driving range, there's nothing to prevent you from doing it.

- A home office needn't be elaborate to be functional. You can decide for yourself if a certain amount of remodeling or redecorating is called for — or if a corner of the dining room table is all you really need in the beginning.

- Working late is easier. So is taking calls before or after-hours, which can be especially important when your customers or suppliers are located in a different time zone.

- You can dress any way that's comfortable. Your phone customer won't have a clue that you're still wearing a robe and houseshoes at 9 a.m.

- You can better manage (or juggle, as the case may be) your work and family obligations. Era Triggs is one of the many who feel that working at home is more efficient. Pointing to her purse-size appointment book she says "As small as this book is, I work out of it. I can take it down to the kitchen and take calls on my business line while I'm cooking. I have the option of never losing business because I'm not at the office when a customer happens to call. And, on the other hand, I'm not sitting at the office on a dead afternoon when I could be getting things done at home."

- One thing peculiar to service businesses is that clients tend to call after hours and on weekends. As any doctor or plumber will tell you, emergencies have a tendency of occurring at times other than normal business hours. A home office allows you to be more accessible.

- Working at home can pull a family closer together by uniting family members in a common project. Children can fully understand what their parents do for a living, instead of growing up with only a vague notion of what happens at some distant office.

Of course, there are potential disadvantages to working at home as well as advantages. To decide if the disadvantages will be serious for your situation ask yourself the following questions.

1. *Will I feel isolated?* Carol Rasmussen, who has a home-based writing and editorial service, explains the problem of feeling disconnected from colleagues. "You never have that much communication with your peers. You're not out there talking to other editors. When you have a problem, you solve it yourself. You don't have anyone you can call and say, 'Hey, what am I going to do about this sentence; it's just not working out and I don't know what the author means.' I miss that."

   One way to overcome this problem is to consciously establish a network of people you can bounce ideas off of, who can offer constructive criticism and advice.

2. *Can I motivate myself to work in an unstructured, un-supervised environment?* Some people find the comforts of home just too distracting, while others thrive there. Will you be bothered by the household chores that need doing? One man solved the problem by a kind of "mental com-muting." Walking out the front door at precisely 8:30 each morning, briefcase in hand, he would walk around to the back door, into his basement office and get down to work.

3. *Will I feel out-of-place among my colleagues and neighbors who still hold regular jobs? Will I feel the need to constantly explain that I "really am working"?*

4. *Will I be able to separate my work from my personal life?* With late calls and customers dropping in unexpectedly, it can seem that you can "never get away from it." One woman, feeling oppressed by the constant sight of her

paperwork, found it helpful to put all of her work out of sight from time to time. An answering service can provide a respite from interruptions when you need a break, and you can avoid publishing your home address, if necessary, to cut down on drop-ins.

5. *Will my spouse and children be supportive?* Friction might arise if, for example, one partner wants to play the stereo while the other is working. Children can resent not being allowed to interrupt a parent working at home.

You'll have to weigh the advantages against the disadvantages for yourself. If you can engineer a workable way of doing it, costs and risks can be drastically cut by working at home.

Key Number 3 — Do Your Own Simplified Market Research

Market conditions were mentioned as one criteria for choosing the right business. It's not enough just to know that there is enough of a market to support your business, however; you must also know the characteristics of your market so you can develop a plan for effectively reaching your customers.

What is market research? Basically it is fact gathering in order to obtain information about your customers — their lifestyles, attitudes and buying habits — that will aid you in directing your business. The more information you have about your market, the better your business decisions will tend to be. Bad decisions, of course, can be extremely expensive when you're in business for yourself.

Market research doesn't have to be an elaborate, expensive production in order to be effective, and it's not beyond the scope of the small independent business. While some kinds of market studies warrant hiring a professional agency, most can be done in a "cheap and dirty" manner in which you do most of the investigative work yourself. That doesn't mean you can afford to be haphazard. Talking to a few customers, your spouse, a few people at a party — and then making a decision is not market research.

You'll need to be much more systematic in your approach.

You can start by making a list of all the questions and problems for which you need answers. At this stage, don't concern yourself with whether or not it will be possible to find the answers, just brainstorm about what information would be most helpful and get the questions down on paper. For example, you'll probably want to know your customer's age group and marital status, along with his occupation and income level. What is his neighborhood like? Are there children in the family? Two wage earners? How often does he travel? What kinds of services, both competing and non-competing, does he presently use? Any of these variables, and many more, can have a bearing on how to most effectively (and inexpensively) approach your customers.

Some of the information you need may be readily available at a local public or college library. Among the resources which can prove helpful are the following:

- *U.S. Census Bureau* publications provide population surveys, furnish information on age, income, size of household, etc. The Bureau also publishes reports on agriculture, construction, housing, and selected service industries.

- *Ayer Directory of Publications* lists trade publications in your field. *The Encyclopedia of Associations* lists the associations that serve your industry. Trade associations and trade publications can be valuable sources of market data.

- *Polk's Directory* contains information secured by an actual door-to-door canvass, listing the names and addresses of all businesses and individuals age 18 and over residing within a certain area. Each listing includes the resident's name, spouse's name, address, occupation, employer, designation as householder, resident or roomer, etc.

  The directory also furnishes helpful facts about businesses within the canvass area, such as firm names and addresses, names and titles of officers and partners, and types of products or services offered.

If you want to concentrate your marketing efforts on a certain neighborhood or district within your community, you can turn to the street directory. There, names are organized according to street name and address. The listings in this section will indicate whether the individual is a homeowner or apartment dweller. Office buildings, as well as types of businesses or professions, are designated.

• Your *Chamber of Commerce* may be able to provide additional information on your target area and on business conditions in your community in general.

Once you've gathered some meaningful information on the demographics you're dealing with you can go to individuals with specific questions. Check the Yellow Pages for other businesses like yours to find out what they charge and how they reach their customers. If your competitors aren't willing to share trade information with a potential competitor you can go outside your area and talk to non-competitors.

The fastest, cheapest way of getting answers only your customers can provide is to conduct a telephone survey. You can write out the survey questions and do the calling yourself or hire a specialized agency to do the calling for you.

Another approach to gathering information from your customers is to use a mail questionnaire. A typical mail questionnaire package consists of a cover letter, a stamped, self-addressed envelope, and the questionnaire itself.

Not everyone will fill out and return your questionnaire, of course, but the more people that do, the better your research results will be. To increase the response rate make your questions seem relevant and important to the group you're mailing to. The cover letter should be friendly and point out how the questionnaire relates to the needs of the recipient. The questionnaire itself should be designed to be interesting, fun, short and to the point, and you should make it clear that respondents will remain anonymous.

Key Number 4 — Subcontracting

If you can subcontract rather than hire employees for your business, at least in the beginning, you'll probably be far better off.

It's easy to underestimate the cost of employees. There is a tendency to think only of the actual wage or salary involved and to overlook such things as the extensive paperwork and bookkeeping, supervision and training, Workman's Compensation, unemployment insurance and other expenses employees involve.

Federal agencies such as the Internal Revenue Service establish guidelines for determining whether a helper is, indeed, an employee or a subcontractor. The determining factors have to do with the amount of supervision, who determines the work schedule, and the method of payment. Generally speaking if you have someone helping you who works at his or her own pace, at the hours he or she chooses, and is paid by the job or on a commission basis or is a member of a profession that charges by the hour, that helper can probably be considered a subcontractor. Government guidelines can change from time to time, however, so you should check the current regulations on this.

Key Number 5 — Define Your Business Broadly in the Beginning

While there can be definite advantages to specializing in your business, you'll probably be better off taking a generalist approach in the beginning.

The decision to specialize should not be based on an arbitrary judgment but on feedback from your particular market. Suppose, for example, that you are starting a word processing service. Your market research makes it clear that there is demand from two distinct markets — the university community and the business community. You could choose to specialize in thesis work, for example, directing all of your promotional efforts at this particular market.

The best way to find out if such a specialized approach is justified is to let your market tell you so. Direct some inexpensive promotional efforts to both markets and compare the responses you get. You may find that the advantages of specializing in thesis work (long-term projects with relatively few clients) are completely outweighed by the demand for business word processing (which can be more lucrative on a per-job basis).

It is also important to keep in mind that the competitive strengths of a small service business lie in its inherent flexibility and capacity for quick response to changing market conditions. Because you're not laden down with costly inventory, office equipment and excess personnel, you can respond to — and profit from — a new opportunity while your larger competitors are still trying to agree on a strategy.

Our high-tech culture is changing almost faster than business can keep up. If a firm becomes too narrow in its vision, too locked into one approach to meeting a need, it can find itself left in the dust of obsolescence. The experience of the railroad industry provides an instructive example. At one time this industry was the largest in the U.S. economy, and industry leaders were confident that their power would never be successfully challenged. Their downfall was simply that they didn't define their business broadly enough. By defining their business as the *railroad* business, rather than the *transportation* business, they were unable to comprehend the incredible new opportunities open to them in such areas as air freight and trucking.

The lesson to be learned from the railroad industry is simply to define your business broadly and stay ever-alert to changing market conditions.

A certain amount of risk is involved in starting any small business venture. Success is rarely a miracle or a fluke, however. By fortifying a good idea with simple business practices like the ones described in this chapter you can vastly improve your chances of success.

Chapter 3
Research and
Information Services

*"The new source of power is not money in the hands of
a few but information in the hands of many."*
— John Niasbitt, *Megatrends*

*"It's very exciting to be involved in a field that is so
new. There are a lot of standards that haven't been set,
hence a lot of opportunities for establishing new ways of
handling information. The field is so dynamic that I
can't imagine ever being bored with it!"*
— Jeanne Raudenbush
President, Information Management Specialists

Information is rapidly becoming recognized as *the* strategic
resource in today's society. Even now there is no shortage of people
who will pay for help in finding, organizing and otherwise
manipulating information. What this means is that a wide open
market exists for your services if you are skilled in working with information — or have the interest and willingness to develop such
skills.

New Careers in Information

Information Brokering

"Probably the most critical thing right now, in this age of information pollution, is having access to the *right* information," says Cassandra Geneson, head of Information Brokers. For example, no one today should think of launching a new business, large or small, without first researching the current state of that industry in depth. "That means asking some key questions," says Cassandra. "For instance, if you want to open up a flower shop, you'd better know how many flower shops there are in your city, and whether it can support another one. And you would do that not by seat-of-the-pants research but by going into the literature — whether it's newspapers or magazines, or maybe going to trade associations — and finding out who's who in your industry."

Exactly what do firms like Cassandra's do? Information brokers conduct secondary research (that is, they research already published data) in order to supply their clients with "strategic" information. They find the answers to questions like "how many subscribers to the *Los Angeles Times* live in Jackson County?" or "What percentage of cosmetics sales are made in department stores?" Not that Cassandra, herself, knows all the answers, but she knows where to *look* for the answers. Her staff of four former librarians extract information from public and university libraries, government archives and trade association files. Cassandra also uses computers to access over 300 on-line data bases, ranging from chemistry and geology to files produced by Dun & Bradstreet. It's her knowledge of how to tap these resources that allows her to provide people in business, industry and the professions with the facts they need to make educated decisions.

It's important to note that the need for strategic information is not limited to business. Virtually anyone can benefit from access to the right information, and that means there is an almost infinite market for research and information skills.

Information brokering businesses generally offer some combination of the following services:

- *Document Delivery*
  Suppose a writer, doing research for an article on current lifestyles among the Apache Indians, wants to find out about educational programs for Native Americans. An information broker can, in a matter of a few minutes, conduct a computerized search of the indeces of some 30,000 magazines and journals for articles on the subject, pull the specific articles the writer needs, and deliver photocopies to him — usually within 48 hours.

- *Selective Dissemination of Information (SDI)*
  The writer in the above example may want to stay informed of new develpments so he can write a follow-up article at some point in the future. By storing the original search strategy with the relevant on-line data bases, the information broker can arrange to have any newly available information automatically sent to his client. In effect, this amounts to a highly specialized and personalized news service.

- *Patent Searching*
  An inventor can see whether his invention is patentable by having a search conducted on the data base files maintained by the U.S. Patent Office.

- *Expert/Speaker Identification*
  Suppose a frozen foods producer wants to create a new line of Chinese foods and needs an expert to develop the recipes. Or suppose an attorney needs an expert witness for an upcoming case involving a highly technical type of product liability. An information broker can help in either situation by locating the names of experts with the necessary qualifications.

- *Instant Briefing*
  In today's increasingly competitive job market, applicants are frequently expected not only to be qualified,

but also to be familiar with a company's background and current projects. You could provide your job-hunting client with comprehensive information on a company or industry. You should realize that this service is in no way limited to helping people looking for jobs, however.

- *Seminars*

    Although there is a growing awareness of the need for strategic information among business and professional people, the vast majority are baffled by the superabundance of resources. Dealing with the materials at the average public library can be frustrating and unproductive for many people. Cassandra Geneson offers a 4-hour "Seminar for Success" wherein she teaches participants how to "walk into a library and not be freaked-out by the multitude of tools."

As with many other services, however, the question is often not whether your client is *capable* of doing the job he's paying you to do but whether he *wants* to do it. As Cassandra points out, it may not be worth his time to do research that you can do much faster, easier and more thoroughly. "When somebody's getting paid four or five hundred dollars a day, you don't want them bouncing off the walls in a library — it's wasting money. And because they don't tend to be very well versed in it, their frustration level is real high; usually they don't like to do it. When we go in, we know exactly what we need to get and how to get it, and if it's not there we know who to contact. If it's not on the shelf for us, that doesn't stop us; we can go to six other places to look for something. We'll take it to the ends of the Earth — we'll know the item does not exist before we stop — and sometimes knowing that information on a topic does not exist is just as important as finding something."

Information Management: Order Out of Chaos

"Records Management" may sound a bit exotic but it actually describes a very down-to-earth, almost universally needed service:

helping people keep track of the information needed to operate their businesses. Whether it amounts to a gardener's few dozen contracts and billing statements, or a doctor's vast accumulation of patient histories, treatment records, insurance reports, professional correspondence and medical journals, paperwork is an increasingly demanding fact of commercial life. Records management specialists help clients to organize their paperwork in such a way that it becomes an accessible tool instead of an overwhelming burden.

Jeanne Raudenbush is president of Information Management Specialists, a firm whose consultants not only help clients bring their inhouse information under control, but also shows them how efficient management of their records systems can result in an improved bottom line. The service might include looseleaf filing; weeding, cataloging and indexing of collections of reports; help with space planning; and actually building an on-line data base of the company's reference materials. IMS might also train the company's support staff to use the records system once it's set up. "We're selling our knowledge," says Jeanne, "our ability to recognize what their records requirements are."

Market Research

Businesses of all types have gradually become aware that they can reduce risks and increase profits by studying and understanding consumer needs and preferences. Market research provides answers to questions about these needs and preferences: What products do consumers buy? How do they like them? When do they buy them? How are the products used? How can the products be improved?

Suppose a company decides to introduce a new hand and body lotion for women. It might begin by packaging a small, sample test batch and having a couple of television commercials made, each with a different approach to selling the new lotion. With a relatively small investment in product development and advertising — and some market research — the company could find out a great deal about the lotion's chances of success and the best approach to marketing the product.

It is at this stage that a *marketing research supplier* could be called on by the lotion manufacturer. Michael Hamilton, who operates his own one-man consulting firm, is an example of such a supplier. Hamilton would first arrange to meet with the lotion manufacturer to determine what information is required and decide what kind of study would be most effective. He would then design all the "instruments" of the study: the type of interview to be used, the actual questions, and the standards for selecting subjects to be interviewed. Finally, he would subcontract with a *marketing research facility*, which is essentially an interviewing service, to actually gather and interpret the data and report back with the results.

"We speak to people in all walks of life and ask them about everything from their automobiles to their chewing gum," says Ruth Nelson of Colorado Marketing Research Services. Her company leases office space in a large mall where a staff of interviewers regularly conduct consumer interviews and record the results. In addition to the mall interviews, CMRS also gathers information by getting consumers together in small discussion groups — called focus groups — and by going door-to-door with interview questions.

Personal interviews are just one method of gathering data about consumers. Another method, especially favored in studies where speed is essential, is the telephone survey, now made even faster by the addition of computer technology. Clare Brown is a pioneer in this area. Her company, Clare Brown Associates, was the first market research facility in the country to computerize its telephone survey operation. "Our interviewers do not, as is typically the case, have a clipboard and a pencil. They're stationed at computer terminals. The question comes up on the screen and they directly enter the response they get by telephone."

Probably the most attractive aspect of the opportunities in market research is the extreme flexibility where scope of operation is concerned. The size of your business can vary depending on what part of the research process you want to enter and what kind of client you want to pursue. Some market researchers, like Michael Hamilton, are quite content to maintain one-person operations; others, like Clare, started out with very modest goals but make the decision to expand once their businesses are up and running. Clare was a little astonished at how quickly her business grew. "This was supposed to be just some little thing where I freelanced a job every once in a while, and before you knew it I had sixteen people working in the attic."

The Nuts and Bolts of Information Businesses

Start-up Costs

The good news about research services is how little start-up capital is required. Most information providers have initial investments of less than $1000, and a surprising number get started with virtually *no* money out of pocket. While it's true that information brokers — like most other new businesses — ordinarily don't turn a profit in the first six to twelve months, the success rates are good — a fact due, in part, to uncommonly low overhead. When Clare Brown set up her operation in a hall bedroom of her home, her only assets were a used typewriter and the attache case given to her as a going away present by her former boss. Within two weeks she had landed a $7000 marketing research contract. "That's the beauty of any service business," says Clare. "I was selling me and my expertise." Jeanne Raudenbush had essentially the same beginning. "Basically, we have never capitalized the business. At first we did it out of the house and out of the car. We lugged the typewriter around."

Data Collection Methods

How will you go about finding information for your client? That will depend largely on his particular needs, but here are the most commonly used resources:

- *Public Libraries.* Generally there are no restictions placed on professional researchers, and reference librarians will often go out of their way to help another information professional.

- *University Libraries.* Living near a university can be a tremendous asset.

- *Your own in-house library.* As you complete jobs for clients you should keep files of your search strategies and the results. Eventually your in-house records will be a valuable reference source.

- *Government archives and agencies.* Over fifty federal agencies routinely gather data on private and publicly owned companies, for example, and much of this information is available without charge.

- *Telephone surveys*

- *Personal interviews*

- *On-line searching*

Since tapping these resources requires considerable time and brainpower, expansion may quickly become an option you'll need to think about. You may, like Michael Hamilton or Kenneth Wilson, elect to remain a one-person operation, working at your own pace, keeping overhead down, operations simple, and minimizing management headaches. Although you may need additional help for larger, more extensive research jobs, that doesn't necessarily mean hiring a full-time staff. Clare Brown, for instance, carried no payroll at first. Instead, she hired interviewers as needed, on an hourly basis.

Records management consulting, on the other hand, does require a somewhat more permanent staff to work with clients on an extended, much more personal basis. Says Jeanne Raudenbush of IMS, "I think it takes more than one person to tackle the legal department of a major corporation. We have about twelve employees, mostly librarians. Some are out running law libraries and technical libraries for our clients; others do looseleaf filing or document delivery. The rest of the staff does records management consulting or market research. Some are part time, as needed; some are full time, salaried.''

Costs of On-line Searching

Until recently, the use of data bases was considered pretty esoteric, limited as it was to scientific researchers and a few graduate students who could afford to use computers as a short cut for their thesis research. In the last few years, however, competition among growing numbers of data base vendors has forced prices down, making on-line searching feasible for many more applications. Today, about half of all information brokers offer this service.

Accessing data bases is still not exactly cheap — the rates may range from $25 to $150 per on-line connect hour. But since a computer can search through an index with incredible speed, the cost can be easily justified. As Cassandra Geneson puts it, "One minute of on-line search time represents one hour of manual digging for information.'' Since connect-time charges are passed on to your clients, your ability to find the right information quickly is of critical importance. That means knowing how to efficiently search data bases, which is mostly a matter of choosing the best key access words. Richard Ross of Information Finders makes a couple of suggestions toward this end:

- Sit down with your client and get him to be as specific as possible about his information needs.

- Use a thesaurus. You can start with a general one, then move to volumes on specific topics.

- Have a search strategy clearly in mind before going on-line. (You may have to alter your strategy depending on the results you get, but at least you'll have a plan to start with.)

Part of being a good searcher is knowing which data bases to access, a skill, says Cassandra, which comes with experience.

"Recently, I did a search for an inventor. He was sitting here while I did the search, and he insisted that I search only the patent file. I said, 'Well, I really don't like to do that because often things are discussed in the engineering or electronics literature that might be in some way related, however remotely, to what you're doing.' We sort of bickered about it, but I wasn't going to let him talk me out of it. The upshot was that we found something — not in the patent file, but in the engineering literature — that was so similar to the design he had in mind, that he realized his idea was not patentable." Cassandra's expertise, of course, had saved him considerable time and money. This also demonstrates the value of being tactfully assertive with your clients.

Equipment Costs

Back in the fifties when Clare Brown launched her marketing research facility, it was quite acceptable to gather and tabulate data by hand. Such was the state of the art. The past thirty years, however, have brought profound changes in the way we do things, and research services have ridden into the 80s on a wave of computer technology. While it's entirely possible to start up in your own home with a minimum of office equipment, you'll need a certain amount of electronic support in your operation in order to be competitive. Fortunately, it doesn't take much, and what is required is not too expensive.

You probably won't need a lot of computing power at home because the computers you'll access are extremely powerful. If you have a home computer, you can adapt it for use as a terminal for around $200 to $400. Alternately you can rent a terminal for about $150 a month or buy one for $400 to $2500. These prices are subject to change, of course, as the prices of all types of computing hardware decline.

Photocopy equipment is nice to have, but it's usually not absolutely essential. Some information providers use coin-operated machines at libraries or take their work to self-service copy shops. If you feel you must have a machine in-house you can rent one for $50 to $400 per month or buy one for as little as $2000.

The Home/Office Debate

Information brokers can and do cut costs — often dramatically — by working at home. "That is one reason we're able to keep our prices very reasonable," says Cassandra Geneson. "Because we work mostly in the field, I don't need a receptionist or an office to receive people. Most of our work is done over the phone and through the mail, so I've been able to eliminate that enormous overhead. It's nice to have a big fancy-shmancy office, but somebody pays for it and it's usually the customer." Again, records management consulting, with its corporate and government clientele, calls for a different approach. Jeanne Raudenbush feels it's important to have an office with an established, professional ambiance, something like a law office. "I think the credibility of having an office, a staff, actually having a ten-year history, is an asset in getting the larger jobs. I think it helps when you're bidding against another firm or against an individual working out of his home." In any case, you'll have to make your own decision about whether the added expense of an office is warranted.

What To Charge Clients

One difficulty in establishing fees is that the field of research and information services is too new to have many precedents. It can be difficult to determine the value of your service to your clients and to decide what you should charge. As Jeanne Raudenbush explains, "I think that information is a commodity we've come to think of as being free, basically, because of the wonderful public library system in this country. Doing research and delivering articles and books to people is something that people are just now accepting having to pay for. You must decide what the value is and how it should be reflected in your charges to the client. I mean, if you can save the client twenty thousand dollars by just spending a couple of hours with him, what is that couple of hours worth? Is it worth just the hourly rate, or is it worth more than that? That's a continuing dialogue we have here, in terms of how we should adjust our rates and how much we should charge clients." For the time being, your fees will probably best be determined by the going rates in your area for the particular service you provide.

- Market research facilities bid on individual projects, basing their charges on an estimate of how many hours and how many interviewers it will take to complete the survey questionnaire. Rates vary between $15 and $75 per hour.

- On-line searchers charge between $25 and $40 per hour for accessing data bases and generally stipulate a one-hour minimum.

- Document delivery prices range from $5.25 to $7.50 per article, plus photocopying and royalty charges. Kenneth Wilson recommends that you make allowance in your prices for extra costs like postage, rush delivery, and parking, all of which can quickly add up. It's a good idea to provide your clients with a detailed, itemized list of these extra charges.

- In records management, a bid is based on how long a job is likely to take, judging from the complexity of the client's organization and its volume of paperwork. For example, a company that does a lot of government contract work and is therefore audited by state and federal agencies, would be likely to have a mountain of forms and records to keep track of. An extensive library system would be required to keep everything easily accessible.

Billing and collecting from your clients can consume as much as 10 percent of your entire operating budget. One way to reduce your invoicing costs is to bill your clients once a month. Once you're established, you might want to arrange deposit accounts for some of your customers (against which you would charge for your services). A deposit account of around $100 is considered reasonable, and can dramatically reduce your billing headaches.

Another possibility is a retainer arrangement, which provides a more predictable cash flow and encourages the client to continue to use your services. Offering your retainer clients discounts on certain services would be a further incentive. Typical retainers are $150 to $250 per month, but they can be as little as $75.

Advertising and Promotion

Once you get started, you'll be likely to find that most of your business comes from repeat customers and referrals. It stands to reason, therefore, that the close personal rapport you establish with your clients — and the word-of-mouth referrals that rapport generates — will become your best advertising tools. It can be frustrating, however, to rely solely on word-of-mouth because it is not something you can easily control. These ideas can help push things along:

- *Brochures*
  Because this field is so new, it's often necessary to actually spell out what your services are and explain to potential clients how you can help them to achieve business goals. Sharp, professional-looking promotional material can say a lot about your company, and the expense is reasonable.

- *Follow-up calls*
  Cassandra Geneson offers a free consultation. This involves going to the client's office for an hour or so and helping him to define his needs. By developing an understanding of the client's problems she is able to submit a proposal outlining solutions she can provide.

- *Professional memberships*
  Professional organizations can provide an opportunity to do some soft selling while keeping you informed of the latest developments in your field. Clare Brown believes professional associations like the American Marketing Association are excellent sources of contacts and referrals. "It's a place to meet prospects in a nonthreatening at-

mosphere. You know, it's a lot easier to chat about your business when you're sitting next to someone at lunch as opposed to calling him up to say, 'Can I come in next week and tell you about my services?' "

- *Directory listings*
  You can have your business listed in one of your local trade directories, such as The Green Book, issued by the New York chapter of the American Marketing Association.

- *Newspaper and radio ads*
  Although her first seminar was a raging success, Cassandra found the newspaper advertising to be extremely expensive. "If we had to do it again that way, we'd have to raise the price, and that's something we'd rather not do." A much better alternative, she feels, would be to get a group — perhaps a women's network or an agency — to sponsor the seminar, guarantee a given number of registrants, and take care of publicizing the event themselves. Radio ads are not generally cost-effective for this type of specialized service.

Perhaps the most important decision you'll face, regardless of the type of advertising you choose, will be how to spend your marketing time appropriately — where to focus your efforts. Jeanne Raudenbush points out, "Very often, one of the mistakes in service businesses such as this is you spend twenty or thirty hours trying to get a $5000 job whereas you may spend an hour or two getting a $50,000 job. You may make a firm decision whether or not to bid on government jobs, because they're very costly to bid on, and you're always bidding against a fairly large field of people. Plus, it takes so much paperwork just to make the submission. You go through a lot of situations like that, and you usually learn the hard way whether or not you're going to go after that end of the business."

Training and Qualifications

Research and information services are more technical than any of the other services covered in this book. The majority of people in this field have degrees in library science or a related discipline. Jeanne started with a bachelor's degree in botany and a master's in library science; while earning her library degree, she worked at Harvard University's Arnold Arboretum Library doing lab and engineering work. Cassandra Geneson worked as a university science librarian for seven years before starting her own business. In the 1950s, when Clare Brown put together her firm, market research was so new that schools hadn't begun to answer the need for training. Clare relied on her experience as an administrative assistant at first; as she was able to take math and marketing courses, she immediately applied her new knowledge in her own business. Today, she feels the ideal preparation would be a double major in marketing and entrepreneurship. That, she says, plus actual hands-on experience working for someone in the field.

Michael Hamilton got started in just that way. After completing his degree in psychology, he took a job with a small marketing research company where he went through an apprenticeship. As he established connections with clients who were his responsibility, he let them know he'd be going into business for himself and asked them to keep him in mind for future projects.

If a four-year degree isn't an option for you, however, don't give up. A good list of training programs can be found in the *Information Market Place* (see appendix).

One last tip from Clare Brown: "Do it a step at a time — don't plunge. By all means, work for someone else in the business so you really see from the inside what's going on. And don't be afraid to ask questions. People love to give advice no matter how high their station in life."

Potential Drawbacks

> "You must recognize that there's never a turn-off. It's like having a child: twenty-four hours a day, seven days a week, you're thinking about this business."

> — Clare Brown

As with any other business, a research and information service creates a burden of decision-making responsibility that is more or less constant. Sharing the load can ease the strains that tend to dilute the pleasures of owning your own business. "One thing that I rejected all along, says Clare, "was to consider a partner, and maybe that was not smart. Now, I think if you could find the right, compatible person that you trusted, it would be a good idea. You could go on a vacation and have peace of mind." Another advantage to having, if not a partner, at least some kind of staff support, is the day-to-day creative interaction with others. Jeanne Raudenbush believes having other points of view is a great help in deciding how to approach a project. "You bring a lot of creativity to the particular jobs, in terms of how you'll handle this kind of litigation or this kind of claim. We've found it very helpful, now that we have a large staff, to be able to sit down and say, 'Well, if I did it this way, what would the problems be?' rather than to sit there and make all these decisions as a single individual."

As previously mentioned, the newness of this field is another potential problem. People have a natural skepticism toward anything which is unfamiliar, and this can be a real problem when your potential clients don't recognize their own needs for your services. Jeanne finds it's often the company boss who's the hardest to sell on the idea of records management. Because the burden of finding company documents falls on the staff, the boss can be almost totally unaware of existing problems. "He doesn't know it took Harry two weeks to locate a particular document because they have a really bad records system. All he knows is that he got that piece of paper, and that's all he cares about. However, if he goes to court and can't find the document he needs to support his case, he recognizes that need very quickly." You may find that a good part of your marketing involves consumer education.

Every field has potential problems, of course, but there are advantages to research and information services as well. There is the excitement of being in a new industry with tremendous growth potential, and there is the gratification of seeing your clients benefit in a tangible way from your services. "Having happy, satisfied clients is a great reward," says Jeanne, "especially if you really make a difference in their overall productivity. I'm surprised at the number of 'atta boys' we get from happy and grateful clients.''

Chapter 4
Child-care Services

"With the number of women who work and have children today, there is a need for 50,000 day-care centers. There are only 9,000 in the whole country."
— Tricia Fox
quoted in *Venture* magazine

Tricia knows what she's talking about when she makes statements like the one above. When she and her husband were unable to find the type of day care they wanted for their children, Tricia left a well-established career selling computers to start Fox Day Schools, Inc. Five years later, she operates six day-care centers, has plans for opening five more in the near future, and is looking into franchising her business in some 40 states. With revenues from her centers already amounting to well over a million dollars, Fox Day Schools is clearly a success.

Child care offers outstanding opportunities for going into business today. In 1980 there were 7.5 million young children with working mothers. By 1990 there will be 10.5 million of these children — a 40 percent increase.

Obviously someone must tend these children in the absence of their parents. A high school-aged babysitter, who'll keep an eye on the kids for a couple of hours after school, will be just fine for some families. Others will find that nothing short of a full-time, live-in nanny will do. But for the majority, the most practical solution lies somewhere in between the sitter and the nanny, and as a result the day-care business is booming today. While most people don't start a day-care center solely because of the financial potential involved, there is good money to be made. If you have a good head for business and love working with children, a day-care business could be the start of a fulfilling and surprisingly profitable career.

The Importance of Attitude

Rosalie Houghton is the quintessential grandmother of the 80s. Tall, trim, with sparkling grey eyes and short, curly hair, she's gentle but spunky. Working with preschoolers is a natural for Rosalie, whose training is in elementary education and whose special interest is in early childhood development. Nineteen years ago she was a young mother herself. With four children — her youngest a kindergartner — she needed a part-time job that would provide an income, an outlet for her skills, and the flexibility she needed for family life. Teaching 2-, 3- and 4-year-olds three mornings a week proved to be just the thing. That was in the '50s. Her children are grown now and she no longer needs a part-time job, but her enthusiasm for working with young children is still strong. Today she serves as director of the Denver Co-operative Preschool. While she loves teaching and co-ordinating the program, no small part of her enjoyment is in helping her staff — nearly all of them young parents themselves — find the same satisfaction she gets in the field.

Rosalie is quick to point out the importance of approaching day care with the right priorities and motivations. "It can be enormously successful, financially, if a person goes into it well planned and with the right attitude. By that I mean, 'I'm going into it because I like children and I have children of my own who will benefit

from the friendships they can make with these day-care children.'
If you're doing it for the money *only*, it can really harm the
children who are with you."

As a care giver, you'll be dealing with the human personality at
a time when it is extremely fragile and malleable. It's during these
first few years that the child begins to acquire — mainly from the
adults who care for him — a critical self image and sense of his
place in the world. Every adult has his own memories of the people
who influenced him as a youngster: the teacher with the kind voice
and the soft lap who noticed the first time he successfully tied his
own shoelaces, as well as the scowling, irritable giant who scared
him half to death. The best way to ensure that *your* influence is
positive and affirming is to prepare yourself with good training, the
best possible working situation and an awareness of the potential
pitfalls.

Preparing Yourself

"I think the most difficult thing is that you're dealing with lots
and lots of individuals," says Rosalie. "Most businesses in the
home are you, one adult, working either independently or with
another adult. Child care involves so many other people." Parents,
helpers, city inspectors and licensing agents, your day-care
children, your own children — in the course of an average week
your public relations skills will get a thorough workout. You'll
need to find ways to minimize the pressures of running your center
so that you maintain the serenity necessary to nurture your charges.
Much of that serenity comes with the confidence born of experience, the fact that just about everything that can happen *has*
happened and, somehow, you've survived it. About this, Rosalie is
reassuring: "You learn that you can handle it. Also, as you do it,
you learn so many songs and finger plays — so many tactics, that
you just pull them out without even thinking. It becomes automatic
and effortless." But what do you do until then?

- On-the-job training, if you can get it, is an excellent way to
  practice and learn by watching others. Rosalie feels her

four years as a kindergarten teacher were especially valuable since she, as the youngest of six, had never been around young children except in her college work. As an alternative to professional schoolteaching, many women — and men — serve as volunteer teachers for church auxiliaries and community organizations before launching their own day-care businesses.

- Classes in early childhood development can provide a good foundation and a sense of what you can reasonably expect from a child at a given age. That kind of perspective can save you from becoming exasperated or feeling like a failure the fourth time in a day one of your four-year-olds spills his milk. Check your local community college or adult education facility for class schedules. Many of these courses are offered at night.

- Local associations of day-care providers may be able to steer you toward workshops and publications that could be helpful. Check to see if such a group exists in your community.

- First-aid training is a must. You'll want to become proficient in both CPR and anti-choking procedures. Your local Red Cross unit may offer courses for as little as $12.

- Draw upon your own experience for ideas. If you've been a working parent yourself, for example, you'll have a special understanding of the needs and problems involved.

Fundamentals

Licensing

You may or may not need a license to operate a day-care service in your home, although in most states a license is required if you care for four or more children (including your own). Check with your local health or social services department.

Home Day Care

Do you have a big family room or a basement rec room that could be sub-divided? A fenced backyard with room for a sand-box? If so, you can take advantage of the chance to work at home — minimizing your overhead — without having to leave your own children. In addition, a home-like environment can be a comfort to day-care children and a great selling point to their parents. Your setup needn't be elaborate, but you may need to do some renovating in order to meet licensing standards.

- You'll need to eliminate safety hazards such as shaky stair treads, torn carpeting or falling plaster. Lead paint should never be used on any surface.

- You'll want to provide good lighting, both natural and artificial, without glare. Big windows are wonderful, but it may be necessary to install guards to keep kids from falling out.

- Adequate heating is essential, especially near floors where children sit, crawl and play. Heat sources and hot pipes must be covered.

- If you live in a hot climate, air conditioning will be a blessing. In any case, you will need good ventilation, especially when working on crafts.

- In choosing floor surfaces, some factors to consider are comfort, durability and maintenance costs. Ideally you would have both linoleum and carpeted areas. Linoleum would provide an easy-to-clean surface for crafts and for toys that roll. Soft, resilient carpeting is great for sitting and crawling. Carpet (as well as drapes and floor pillows) also helps keep noise levels down — important for your nerves as well as the kids'.

- You can increase your usable space with platforms, which can be built to contain closets, shelves or drawers for storage.

Furnishings

- Try to get child-sized chairs and tables. If you're handy you can make them yourself easily and cheaply from plywood and cardboard tubes, available at lumber yards and electrical supply houses.

- A big overstuffed chair is great for reading and climbing on. Get a clean used one from Goodwill or the Salvation Army.

- Floor pillows are, of course, a must. If you have the space a giant bean bag is great for jumping on.

- A carpet-lined bathtub can be fun to play in, and it can offer a somewhat secluded spot for reading.

- Room dividers are a convenient way to subdivide space; you can change the arrangements as needed during the day. Four-foot dividers are about the right size because you can look over the tops.

Activities

Creating the program or "curriculum" for your day-care service is where the creativity — and fun — really begin. The first step in planning learning experiences is to simply ask yourself what you want your day-care children to gain from their time with you. You might want to offer a highly structured, teacher-directed program which prepares the children for school, or you might favor the more open, child-directed approach which presents lots of options. Whichever you choose — and even experts can't agree on one "right" approach — you'll want to make sure your program is compatible with the expectations of the families you hope to cultivate as clients. It could be very uncomfortable, if not impossible to operate, if you find yourself at odds with the majority of your clients over basic child-care philosophy. Another thing to keep in mind is that learning is not confined to segments labeled "art" or "science." Everything that happens to a child from the time the carpool drops him off until he leaves your doorstep makes an impression. Each activity, whether it is building a pyramid or putting on galoshes, has the potential for developing new skills which can build the child's feelings of worth and competency.

Although your program needn't be complicated, it should include a science activity, some music, a story, and play that uses the large muscles. Incorporating these four activities into each day's agenda takes no small amount of planning. As Rosalie says, "It's a challenge to sit down and work out a program that takes in all of these. I always did my planning by the semester. You almost have to do that because you have to work in the holidays and seasons, and then you have to figure out how many days you'll need here and there. Some ideas can be finished in a single day. Other ideas will take three days to explore, work on and finish up." At any rate, here are some ideas you can draw from as you create your own program:

- *Opening Hour*

  Since your day-care children will arrive at different times, depending on their parents' schedules, you may want to have a time in the morning that's very loosely organized, perhaps an hour or so of free play, during which you or a helper can greet each child as he or she arrives. This personal recognition serves a double purpose: first, it lets you know who's there and who isn't, and second, taking just a moment with each child to say "Hi. My, that's a pretty shirt!" or "What'd you have for breakfast?" seems to set the tone for the rest of the day. It gives each child a sense that he is important as an individual, and that can be especially helpful if the child happens to arrive in a bad mood. Says Rosalie, "If you can pick up on it right then as they come through the door and maybe give an added hug or added attention, you can often alleviate problems later in the day.'' At the very least, parents should not leave a child at the door, but bring him into an enclosed area where you can see that he has arrived.

* *Housekeeping*
  Always a favorite of both sexes, housekeeping can provide great opportunities for learning social skills. A make-believe stove and refrigerator are nice if you can get them. Other things like small dishes, pots and pans and cookie cutters can be scrounged from your own kitchen discards. Be sure to have a play telephone.

* *Dress up*
  Kids also love to dress up and act out elaborate scenarios. Look through your closets for old hats, shoes and purses. (Parents can also donate to the dress-up wardrobe.) See if you can find a carpenter's apron, a nurse's cap, or fire-fighter's hat, so the kids can act out adult occupations.

* *Music*
  Music can serve several functions: entertainment, tension releaser, and learning tool. Rosalie uses music as a signal and a transition between activities. When it's time to put away the toys and gather for story time, she lets the children know by singing "It's pick-up time, pick-up time." At midmorning, when it's time for a snack, she and her class sing this funny tongue twister:

  > *Hungry, hungry I'm so hungry*
  > *Table, table here I come*
  > *I could eat a goose-moose burger*
  > *Fourteen pickles and a purple plum*

Rosalie explains, "If you simply clap your hands or do some things on the piano, this is an abrupt change and children don't really take to abrupt change. This way, you're not demanding. You're presenting a new phase, and in the length of a song, most children can make the transition from one activity to the anticipation of another.''

- *Toys*
  Blocks made of either wood or sturdy cardboard are practically essential. While the children build their forts and caves with them they acquire physical dexterity and practice conceiving shapes and spacial relationships.

  If you have many rainy days, you'll be grateful for a large tumbling mat upon which the kids can release their pent-up energy.

  Not all toys need to be store bought. Cardboard boxes and paper towel tubes can be cut up and taped together with masking tape to make elaborate structures like multi-level garages and airports. A long piece of cardboard can make a ramp to launch airplanes.

- *Interest centers*
  A reading corner — any fairly secluded and inviting spot — can be created with a piece of shaggy carpet and a big chair or some floor pillows. Ideally books would be kept on shelves or a rack, rather than piled on the floor.

  The science corner should be designed for doing as well as looking. You can equip yours inexpensively with scales for weighing things, measuring tools, a magnifying glass, and some natural objects like rocks, sea shells, and maybe a bird's nest. If you have the space, you might get an aquarium, terrarium, or a guinea pig which your children can help feed and care for.

  A water table can be great fun as well as relaxing for a tense child. Include some cups and funnels for pouring and measuring. If you're adventurous, you might try Rosalie's idea: "We filled a water table with mud. It was wonderfully successful. How many children — except in their sandbox — get a chance to really get into mud?"

A learning center might include puzzles, some building and manipulative toys such as Leggo, Lincoln Logs, pegs or beads, and some educational games.

Math can be taught in simple no-pressure ways like discussing the week's plans displayed on a big calendar with the months and days of the week prominently marked.

- *Meals*

If your day-care hours are short, say two or three hours in the morning or afternoon, a simple snack will do. "Ants-on-a-log" (celery spread with peanut butter and topped with raisins) is an example of a quick and easy but nutritious snack. Add a cup of milk or juice and you're set. If, on the other hand, you plan to offer early-morning to evening care, you'll need to plan for at least one full meal as well as morning and afternoon snacks. Sack lunches are one solution, of course, but it can become monotonous. Even though it means more work for you, homemade meals are probably the better way to go. Some helpful tips:

— Your local USDA extension service can probably help you with meal planning.

— The USDA Child Care Food Program subsidizes meals provided in family day-care homes. If you serve two snacks plus a lunch, for example, you may qualify to receive about $1.50 per child per day to help pay for food. You'll have to keep records of the meals served, however, and they must meet USDA nutritional standards.

— Unless you have a dishwasher, paper plates and cups, which are thrown away after one use, are recommended.

— Make sure to check with parents about food allergies. Sensitivities to milk and wheat are not uncommon.

— If possible, children should be given the opportunity to help with preparation and cleanup.

- *Naps*
  In any program lasting more than four hours a day, you must provide a nap period. You can have the children sleep on cots, or if you have carpet, they can stretch out on mats on the floor. It helps if each child can bring his own mat, rug or blanket from home.

- *Toileting*
  It's important to remember that preschoolers are still in various stages of learning basic hygiene and grooming. Part of your task will be to continue the training they receive at home. Here are some pointers:

  — A bathroom which is well lighted and attractive will make children feel safe and comfortable and, therefore, more inclined to *use* it.

  — Ask parents what words or signs the youngster uses to let them know he needs to use the toilet.

  — Provide steps for sinks and toilet and lowered mirrors so the kids can groom themselves better.

  — Water should be thermostatically controlled; no hotter than 120 degrees Farenheit.

  — Provide paper towels but place the dispenser as far from the toilet as possible. Kids enjoy stuffing paper into the toilet and then watching it flush away.

  — It's better if your day-care children can use a bathroom which is separate from the one your family uses. That way you can control the articles that are kept in the room and eliminate anything dangerous, like razors or cleaning fluids. A separate day-care bathroom will also lessen the spread of illness-causing germs.

- *Illness*
  Naturally, if a child is sick he should be kept at home. Still, you should have a nice place for isolating a sick child, somewhere you can keep an eye on him until his parent can come for him. The area should have a comfortable cot, a few toys or books and should be near a toilet.

Administration and Finances

Before you accept a child into your day-care program, encourage his parents to come, observe and ask questions. There should be a good understanding of your mutual needs and expectations. A parent questionnaire can provide you with valuable information about the child, such as her sleeping, eating and toileting habits. How long does she nap? Does she have any special fears (such as fear of dogs or of lightening)? Is he right- or left-handed? Does he have a security blanket or special toy?

How Much to Charge?

Weekly charges can range from $15 to $100 per week per child, depending upon where you're located and what your service offers. In order to arrive at an equitable fee, estimate the costs of running your business. Make a written estimate covering food, arts and crafts supplies, books and toys, cots, playpens and any other supplies and equipment you'll need. Don't forget the extra utilities and wear and tear on your home. Your fee should also cover the special insurance you'll need for home liability and outings in your car. (Group liability and accident insurance may be available through a day-care association in your area). Last but not least, allow for your own salary.

- Parents might be willing to pay a premium for care in a home with a low adult/child ratio, where each child receives more individual attention.

• Can you afford to waive charges when a child is sick? How about vacations? There are a number of things to consider in setting your fees.

Advertising

Word-of-mouth advertising may be all you need, or you may want to place a note in your local newspaper. You can also post notices on community bulletin boards and let the personnel offices at nearby businesses know you're going into business. If you know of centers with prohibitively long waiting lists they may be happy to refer clients to you.

Emergencies

You will need written permission for emergency medical treatment for each child, and a record of inoculations and allergies is also a good idea. Find out whom you should call if, in an emergency, the parent can't be reached, and get written permission for this individual to pick up the child if necessary. It's a good idea to display your home's emergency procedures in a prominent place.

Hiring Help

If you care for more than six children, you'll definitely need another adult helper. What is the best adult-to-child ratio? The children's ages will be an important factor, but Rosalie recommends three adults for ten children. ''When you think about crossing streets and things, remember you only have actual contact with two children. With three adults, you always have one who can tend to the child who's having problems, whether it's to change clothing or dry tears as his mother leaves — whatever the situation is.'' If a three-to-one ratio seems like a budget-straining luxury, you could compromise by hiring a single helper for when you're at home and only adding additional helpers for outings.

Be selective in making your hiring decisions. Carefully observe how any applicants interact with children. Do they genuinely like kids? Can they be relied upon to exercise mature judgment?

Extended hours will make staggered shifts necessary. Often you can hire highly qualified teachers who want the flexibility of working part-time. "In our school," says Rosalie, "all of our teachers teach part-time, and all but one have children at home. It's a wonderful chance for them to get good teaching experience and still be home when their children are home, available when they're needed."

Avoiding Possible Pitfalls

How do you go about ensuring an atmosphere of order and contentment, where children can feel secure and comfortable? Without question, the first step is to safeguard your own feelings of self-confidence and your sense of controlling the situation. Make sure you have realistic expectations of yourself, your day-care children and your own family.

Rosalie points out the importance of being flexible and having a sense of humor. Flexibility is important because kids are unpredictible and it's often necessary to drop your well planned schedule and do something entirely different. A good sense of humor can keep you from taking things too personally. For example, sometimes children will come in and look at you and say "I don't want to stay." A sense of humor can help you to realize that such comments are directed at the situation rather than at you personally.

Affection can also help you to deal with difficult situations. As Rosalie says, "I give lots of hugs. If I'm feeling tense, if something has gone wrong, or hasn't worked like I thought it was going to . . . I've learned not to dwell upon it. That's the time I will very often just sit down on the floor and ask somebody, 'Would you like to sit on my lap?' and just hug for a few minutes."

For all of its challenges and demands, child care has to be one of the most gratifying occupations imaginable. There is a special pleasure that comes with knowing that you've contributed in some way to the strengths and achievements of another person, that you've influenced his values and given him some good memories. "Oh, there are many, many, many rewards," says Rosalie. "One is knowing at the end of the year that I have offered these children a thousand areas and have let them pick and choose what they wanted to learn. They're bound to learn certain things: maybe that I'm a friend, maybe that they're comfortable in this group of children and can then go on to a bigger group."

Asked what she considered her greatest reward over the years, Rosalie said "Oh, I think the hugs and the sad looks at the end of the year. And when the children come back three years later and they've grown enormously, but when they see you they light up. I've met children who've been out of preschool for ten years and they may not remember what I look like, but when you say to them, 'I'm Rosalie,' they remember the name and they remember it with good feelings."

Chapter 5
Word-Processing Services

The advent of computers has created a wide range of new self-employment opportunities. Computer-based businesses have been formed to maintain mailing lists, manage inventory, and keep track of payroll, expense and maintenance records, among other things.

The single most popular type of computerized business opportunity, however, is surely word processing. Because computers increase the efficiency of working with written documents to a remarkable degree, small word-processing businesses have found a ready market for their services. And within the broad category "word-processing services," there are numerous specialty niches including services to business, academia, and law, engineering and other professions.

Wide Open Opportunities

Opportunities in word processing tend to be unusually open-ended. As the owner of a word-processing service, you're in a unique position to discover opportunities in editing, proofreading, translating, graphic design, copywriting, ghostwriting, research and many other related services. This makes word processing especially appealing if you're the type of person who can respond to new opportunities in an entrepreneurial fashion.

Beverly Shannon's experience offers a case in point. After her 13-year marriage ended in divorce, Beverly found herself alone with three kids and mounting bills. While working at a temporary office personnel firm she noticed the increasing demand for word-processing operators. The potential of the industry intrigued her, and she soon opened "Away With Words, Inc."

Describing the rapid growth of her company in a *Rocky Mountain Business Journal* article, Beverly said: "We started as a service bureau only, but soon we were being asked to provide companies with temporary word-processing operators. Then we were asked to do programming for companies. Then we were asked to do workshops and seminars."

With a client list of several hundred, including companies like Avis Rent-a-Car, Frontier Airlines, and Diners Club International, Beverly's success is impressive. There is more to come, however. Recognizing a need for a high quality word-processing training program, she recently founded the Colorado Business Technology Institute to fill this need. And she's looking ahead to adding a telecommunications system which will allow her client companies to submit their work via phone lines.

One Service Profiled

Of course it's not necessary to grow to the point where you employ several dozen employees, as Beverly's firm does, in order to be successful in the word-processing business. Home-based word-processing services, operated by the owner with few (if any) employees, can also be successful.

Mary Jean Huerta's service, "Word Organizer," is a good example. Located in the former "catch-all room" of her home, Mary Jean's office is sunny and pleasant. The room is filled with parakeet song, the soft whir of disk drives and the quiet clicking of the keyboard.

A degree in microbiology may seem like an unlikely background for the owner of a word-processing service. Mary Jean explains that after graduation she took a job with a lab, expecting to put her education to work. "There wasn't an opening in the back — what they really needed was someone to answer the phones. They told me I'd move back within six months or so, but of course that never happened. It's a myth, you know, that a secretary is going to work her way up. There's nowhere to go except Number One Secretary. Then there was the point where I was putting out five hundred a month for day care. That and taxes took a huge amount of my salary. I ended up making a hundred dollars a week, and I'd come home too tired to do anything else. I was just digging a rut for myself."

Mary Jean got out of her rut. She quickly mastered her company's CPT 8100 computer and made plans to start her own business. Now, at 27, her plans have become reality.

"Like almost all families right now, we need that second income. I'm not getting cabin fever and I don't feel like I'm stifling myself. I still feel like I'm growing. When my children get back into regular school, I feel that I won't have lost my business techniques," she said.

Exactly What Is a Word Processor?

A word processor is a computer with a software program that allows you to produce written communications such as contracts, reports, legal documents and financial statements. The software, together with the computer, printer and other components, make up a "system":

- The keyboard resembles that of a standard typewriter but includes keys for special functions like formating, deleting and inserting text, and printing.

- The CRT, or cathode ray tube, looks like a miniature TV screen. As the operator types, the characters are displayed on the screen.

- Disk drives are the slots into which "floppy disks" are inserted. Floppy disks resemble 45 rpm phonograph records, but are smaller and thinner, and they're made of magnetic recording media. There are two kinds of disks: one contains the software that runs your system; the other stores the documents that you produce.

- The printer looks like a typewriter without a keyboard, and, as its name suggests, it is the component that finally prints your work. Dot matrix printers produce lines and characters with tiny dots, and are essential for printing graphs and diagrams. They are usually much faster than letter-quality printers, which produce individual characters by striking a print wheel, so they are often used for printing first drafts, too. Letter-quality printing is usually reserved for the final drafts of reports, business letters, resumes and other documents.

The feature that most distinguishes a word-processing system from a standard typewriter is its memory — its capacity to store information which can later be retrieved, edited, rearranged or printed. Memory also streamlines and simplifies the actual typing process. When you make a typo on a word processor it is almost effortless to correct it. There's no need to hit the return key when you reach the end of a line of type because that is taken care of automatically. Omitted letters or words — which are difficult to correct on a typewriter and often require retyping an entire page — are a snap with a word processor. And if you misspell a word throughout the text of a document, you can direct the system to "look for" each occurrence of that word and make the necessary corrections. Again, if the correction alters the length of the line, the system automatically compensates for it.

Few typists enjoy the tedious task of centering headings and columns of figures by counting characters. With a word processor, you need only type the heading, then press the centering key, and automatically the heading will be centered. Columns of figures can be automatically tabulated by their decimal points.

If you've ever used the "cut and paste" method to rearrange text, you'll fully appreciate the ease of editing with a word processor. If you want to move a paragraph to another location, for example, you simply indicate what you want moved, then indicate where you want it moved, and with a couple of keystrokes it's done. Only after you're completely satisfied do you press the "Print" button and then sit back while the printer turns out an edited and perfectly typed manuscript.

It's true that certain tasks (short letters and certain kinds of forms, for instance) are still more efficiently done on a typewriter. For the most part, however, word processing produces enormous savings of time and effort. It also makes possible some kinds of communications — "personalized" mass mailings, for instance — that would otherwise not be practical.

Who Needs Word Processing Services?

Word processing is ancillary to writing and editing; logically, anyone with a need for written communication would appreciate having that communication made faster, easier, and cheaper.

Small Business

"The client I prefer to deal with," says Mary, is the independent businessman who is too small to have an office of his own and too big to have his wife do it."

Mary points out that while her service may cost him more per hour than hiring a secretary, it can be much less expensive in the long run. Since she works on a contract labor basis, all the customer pays for is the work he receives. That might amount to $200 or $300 per month, compared with the $800 to $1,200 he'd spend on salary alone for a secretary. (With the addition of taxes, insurance and benefits, his actual outlay might rise to $1,500 or more per month.) Mary's word processing service is a very cost-effective alternative.

Cost savings are not the only benefit to the small businessman, either. Mary speaks of a building contractor client who frequently prepares proposals. "Occasionally he'll just call me on the phone and say, 'Mary, just fill in the blanks here and here on the computer.' I put out a contract that looks like it's been done specifically for that client — it doesn't look like a 'fill in the blanks' proposal."

Writers, Independent Researchers

One of Mary's customers is a geophysicist who writes programs for computers. She has just completed his latest project, a 50-page manual.

"My fee includes one free edit. Once I give him that first draft — on dot matrix — he can correct it, edit it, rearrange it aesthetically, give it back to me and get exactly the kind of paper he wants."

Resumes

Asked how she could afford to compete with the professional resume services, Mary responded: "These ads that say 'Resumes: $9' — that's just for the interview. It runs as much as $100 to have the resume done. I can send them out of here with a good quality resume that I write for $12." How can she afford to do that? "I'm working out of my house. It takes me about an hour to sit down, write, and turn out a complete resume, which they can then take to the printer. For $10, the printer will give them a hundred copies. So, for a total of $22, they can get a resume that would cost a good $100 at a resume service. And it's just because I don't have the overhead.

"Plus, they can sit down and have a cup of coffee and I'll have it out for them in an hour. Resume services will start by interviewing you and you come back the next day or the day after. So if they're in a bind, they can have it in an hour's turn-around.

"I also store their resume for six months at no extra cost, so if they want to have something updated and reprinted at some time in the future, all they need to do is call me and give me the changes and I'll print up the number of copies they need and store it for another six months."

Students

Undergraduate students are generally not likely customers, simply because word processing services charge much more than typists, who can type at home for as little as $1 per page. Graduate students, however, can be a good market for your services. Theses and dissertations often undergo three or four revisions, which makes word processing cheaper — not to mention faster — in the long run. The most time-consuming, and therefore most costly part is the initial inputting of the thesis onto a disk. After that, changes generally require little of the service's time.

Other Markets

The applications possible for your service will be determined by your own experience and interests, together with the types of needs in your area. For instance, one successful nightclub sends a bimonthly newsletter to its customers. The single sheet newsletter is designed, edited and printed on a word processor. Another example is the California woman who started a home business by producing film scripts for local writers. With few exceptions, anything that can be typed can be done more efficiently on a word processor. As more and more people become aware of the benefits of computerization, your business opportunities can only increase.

How To Get Started

Learning to use a word processor is not especially difficult — you don't need to be intimidated by the "bells and whistles." In fact, some systems have become so "user-friendly" that the operator is virtually led by the hand through every step. This isn't to say, however, that you won't need some basic skills in order to make your business a profitable enterprise.

- *You should be able to type by touch.* Technically, it's possible to input a document by fast hunting and pecking, but you will probably find that the computer's speed makes you impatient with doing it that way.

● *Next, you need to learn to operate a word-processing system.* There are any number of ways of doing that, none of which involve enrolling in a long curriculum of math or computer programming, as many people seem to believe.

1. You can learn on the job, working as a word processor operator for a legal firm or any other business where word processing is used. This type of training offers a couple of distinct advantages: you'll be paid while you learn, you'll have a chance to become familiar with the kinds of paperwork used in at least one type of business, and you can apply this knowledge later in your own business.

2. If you can't find an employer who will hire you without previous word processing experience, you can work as a temporary for one of the employment agencies who offer free computer training to clients. At one agency, temporaries are eligible for word processing training after 160 hours — about one month — of regular office assignments. The training is self-taught and requires from six hours to two days.

3. Classes are another option. Secretarial schools, adult continuing education, and even computer stores now offer courses which last from one weekend to a complete semester.

4. Actually, you don't have to take classes or training at all if you're willing to sit down with a manual and teach yourself. It was this approach that Mary took. "I bought this system about eight weeks before starting my business, and I sat down for

eight weeks and just whipped through all the stuff related to the programs. It came with the system. Also, the salesmen make themselves available so they can troubleshoot any problems you have via the phone."

In any case, you don't have to go back to school for a year. Within a month you can learn the basics; speed and skills improve with practice.

- *You'll need a working knowledge of spelling, grammar and punctuation.* Yes, you can simply type your client's copy just as it is given to you, but your ability to edit will, in time, make your service much more valuable to him.

- *You must deliver high quality work, and that means few, if any, typos.* Your work must be done on time and at the price you estimated. If there are problems or factors that change the cost (unreadable handwriting or extensive editing, for example), you must communicate with your client and solve the problem. It's also important that your client understand that "computerized" doesn't mean "magic." He must be given a clear idea of how much time the job will take. Otherwise, he could be expecting the work much sooner than you can deliver and that could damage your credibility.

- *You'll want to cultivate an air of professionalism.* Your services will cost much more per hour or per page than what a typist would charge, and in justifying that price difference, image can be almost as important as the product.

    "You have to be good at public relations, says Mary. "You have to be able to present yourself well to your clients because when they walk into your home they have to know that they haven't just hired some little housewife that's sitting home with her kids, trying to make an extra buck."

"Your phone technique can make or break you. Ninety-nine percent of your customers contact you by phone first, and if you hem and haw and can't quote things right, it won't work. You've got to sell yourself on the phone."

- *You must be able to handle pressure.* There will be rush jobs and the inevitable equipment breakdowns, and you'll need to deal with those situations calmly as they arise.

- *You'll need to be suited to the work.* Can you tolerate long hours of sitting? Can you work alone? Word processing is, for the most part, a sedentary and isolated job. Unless you answered 'yes' to those questions, you could find yourself growing fidgety after awhile.

Choosing a Word-Processing System

Word processing is one of those businesses in which your primary investment is in equipment, rather than in inventory or in long years of schooling. In fact, the business is so dependent on equipment that choosing a system that will reliably do the job might be the most important decision you make. With new computer companies constantly springing up, it can be a difficult decision, and unless you already know quite a bit about computers you're going to need some help. Computer salespeople are often new to the product themselves, in which case they won't be your best resource. The salesman will be able to point out his product's features — emphasizing the advantages while, of course, downplaying the drawbacks — but he won't be able to help you comparison shop. That could mean a lot of store hopping for you, which can quickly turn into a blur of names, brochures and business cards that leave you more confused than when you started. So where do you turn for reliable information? How do you get a handle on what you'll really need? How can you protect yourself from getting a bad deal? A few simple guidelines will help you get started.

• *First of all — and notwithstanding what the salesmen might tell you — there is no such thing as the perfect system.* Each computer has its own strengths, and in choosing one over another, there will always be trade-offs. The trick is to get the system that has the most of what you want for your particular operation. Some systems excell in producing scientific and engineering work, for example, and were specifically designed for this type of work. Other systems are great for working on especially long documents, such as doctoral dissertations. Try to determine what type of work you'll be most likely to get *before* deciding on a particular system.

• *Research the market in your area.* Try to decide what kind of clientele you want to cultivate, then find out what equipment other word processing services are using to do the same kind of work.

   If you hope to get overflow work from other services (it can be a good source of income), your equipment should be compatible with theirs.

   If you plan to produce newsletters, brochures or ads you may want to investigate systems that can display a full page exactly like your layout.

• *Service can be a major consideration.* A leased or rented system usually comes with a service agreement providing for on-site repairs and maintenance. If you buy a system, on the other hand, you'll probably have to take it back to the shop (or ship it back to the factory) for repairs. If you assemble your system yourself from components purchased from a number of different dealers, service can become a serious problem.

   Consumer guides, available at bookstores and libraries, are a good way to learn which systems seem to be relatively trouble-free and which ones have a variety of "bugs." With any luck, the system you fall in love with won't also be the one that's prone to frequent breakdowns.

- The lowest price does not necessarily indicate the best deal. It may be worth a few hundred dollars more to deal with a well established company that has a good track record for customer support.

Financing Options

There are several ways to pay for the system you finally choose; like the computer itself, there are trade-offs with each method.

If your budget is limited, purchasing a system through a bank-financed loan could provide the lowest monthly payments. Another advantage of buying over leasing or renting is that your payments build equity. Payments are higher with a lease or rental agreement; however, these arrangements offer some advantages over buying. First, there is no down payment. Second, if you want to change or upgrade your equipment, you simply trade it back to the company. Finally, while leasing doesn't commit you to purchase the machine, you do, at the end of the lease, have the option of buying for a percentage of the original price.

Other Office Expenses

Fortunately, word processing is one of those businesses that are well suited for the home office. Do you have an extra bedroom or a den that isn't being used? Good! You can enjoy the many advantages — in both cost and convenience — that go with working at home.

- You can work whatever hours are best for you, whether that turns out to be mornings while your children are at school, or late at night, or weekends.

- You can say goodbye to the hassles and expense of commuting, downtown parking, and fast food lunches.

- Business attire is optional — at least when you're not meeting with clients.

- Not only will you pay no additional rent, but a percentage of your existing housing costs can be deducted from your taxable income. This is also true for your utilities and phone service.

- Speaking of utilities, most home-based services experience only minor increases in their electric bills as a result of their system's power consumption. You may want to invest a little money in a "surge suppressor" which can even out the peaks and valleys in your home's electric current. Any type of fluctuation or interruption in the power supply can wreak havoc with your system's memory — as you'll find out yourself the first time your toddler pulls the cord out of the wall socket while you're working. Which brings us to the next point.

- Your work area must be away from distractions. There should be room SOMEWHERE ELSE for youngsters to play. If you have young children in your home, day care or even a mother's helper could provide considerable peace of mind for a few hours each day and will be well worth considering.

- Your office should have good lighting, a roomy work table at a convenient height, and a comfortable (preferably adjustable) chair. The room should also have adequate heating and air conditioning since disks can be sensitive to extremes in both heat and cold.

- You will need a phone in your office, although it can be either a separate business line or just an extension of your home phone. This will allow you to bring up a client's work on your system while discussing it on the phone.

- You'll need to invest in some standard office supplies: stationery, envelopes, at least two grades of paper, business cards. You'll also need supplies specifically for word processing: floppy disks, ribbons and print wheels. A nice added touch is clear plastic covers for your clients' theses and reports.

How To Charge

Some services charge an hourly fee, something between $12 and $15 per hour. Others prefer to charge by the page. Mary-Jean Huerta, for example, charges $4 per page for single-spaced work, $2.75 per page for double-spaced. One edit is included free. If she edits the work herself, or, in the case of a resume, actually writes the document, she charges 50 percent more per page. Any method you choose must cover your overhead and provide for a reasonable profit. When figuring your overhead, be sure to include these items:

- Payments on your equipment, rent, phone and utility expenses

- Supplies, including paper, ribbons and disks. Some services charge clients for a disk with their first job and reserve the disk for any future jobs with that client.

- Your time and expertise. In addition to billable hours, you'll spend a lot of time talking with clients on the phone before the job starts, so take that into consideration.

Check with other word processing services to learn what the going rate is in your area. If you find that other services are able to charge less than you can, you may need to cut operating costs in order to be competitive. On the other hand, you may find that you can provide higher quality service (more competent editing, for example) to justify your higher rates.

Obtaining a refundable deposit before starting a job (especially with a new client) will give you a sense of security about being paid and will reduce the number of last-minute cancellations. The deposit might be fifty cents per page of the work brought to you, or a set percentage of your estimate for the job.

Obtaining Clients

"A good ad" says Mary, is the best way to attract customers to your new business. Although you'll certainly want to investigate advertising in local trade magazines and newsletters, your best bet might be a simple insertion in your local newspaper's classified ads. Mary runs only two lines in capital letters: " COMPUTER PROCESSED TYPING," followed by her name and phone number." Just as important as what the ad says is where it's placed. Placement in the classification with typists and resume services will probably work best for you.

One inexpensive way to advertise is to leave your business card at places your potential clients might go. Print shops and copy shops, as well as bookstores and supermarkets, often have bulletin boards where you can pin a card.

Don't overlook other computer owners; you might be able to do some of their overload work or work their systems can't efficiently handle.

Regular rather than sporadic advertising will bring the most satisfactory results. You'll not only minimize the "when it rains, it pours" problem — too much business at one time, not enough at others — but you'll also be more likely to get the customer who suddenly needs a word processor and remembers seeing your ad. Another benefit of consistent advertising is that it fosters an image of stability, and that is important with any kind of service business.

Finally, there is nothing quite as convincing to a prospective customer as a friend's recommendation of your service. In the long run, word of mouth — referrals from satisfied customers — will be your best form of advertising.

Chapter 6
Catering Services

Secret Service Caterers wasn't a secret very long. In fact, the four-year-old business has proved so successful that its owners, Peggy Davenport and Kathie O'Donnell, are themselves a little amazed. What began as "something to do other than clean the house and go to lunch with friends" has become a popular catering business whose clients include tennis clubs and art museums. The occasion might be anything from a cocktail party to a celebration of Native American culture. "We do it all," they say.

Peggy and Kathie are young, energetic women. Peggy is bubbly and outgoing, Kathie, a little quieter, but they both enjoy talking about their business. They seem delighted with their partnership, finishing each other's sentences as they talk and laughing over their shared adventures. Asked to describe their most interesting party, both agree it had to be the art museum buffet which had the American Plains Indians as its theme. "All our food was based on the food they would have used at the time," explained Kathie. "Buffalo kabobs and wild rice stuffed mushrooms." An overview of other Indian groups, like the Indians of the Pacific Northwest, included salmon. Small, typed sheets told the origins of each dish.

Although the two usually don't get involved in table decorating, this time they fashioned a teepee for the table, and even wore Indian tunics. Tying everything together was challenging and fun.

Creative Catering

Peggy and Kathie are just two of the many ambitious young entrepreneurs who have recognized the growing opportunities in catering. For a number of reasons there has never been a better time for turning a love for cooking and entertaining into a lucrative career. First, there is our new national passion for good foods, as evidenced by the proliferation of gourmet food shops, kitchen equipment stores and gourmet magazines. Cookbooks frequently make the bestseller lists these days. The consumer is definitely open to quality foods today. The second factor, a natural result of our growing culinary sophistication, is that throwing a party has become more complex. You don't just go to the supermarket and pick up a few cans of party nuts anymore. Now, entertaining in style means combing the gourmet shops for baby artichokes and Devonshire cream. Finding the right ingredients is only half the task; it might take hours to prepare that really elegant dinner for six. Even those who have the know-how frequently can't find the time for preparing elaborate meals. The solution, increasing numbers of hosts and hostesses are deciding, is to hire a professional caterer. Still another element in the growth of the catering business is that while people enjoy the convenience of having a professional do the party, they frankly love the personal service. It's wonderful to be able to relax and enjoy the party, knowing that every detail has been taken care of.

In addition to the traditional sources of business — the weddings and anniversaries, the birthdays and bar mitzvahs — you can find a ready market for catering among the following:

- Corporate functions. Caterers are routinely used by businesses for luncheons, cocktail parties and promotional events. Some businesses, such as film crews, find it more efficient and economical to have catered breakfasts and lunches brought in when on location. Businesses generally comprise about 25 percent of the total catering market.

• Charities and cultural groups such as ballet or theater guilds typically hold fundraisers throughout the year. As often as not these are catered events.

• Single professionals and two-career couples increasingly enjoy a homecooked meal brought in. They can afford the price, but can't afford the time to do it themselves.

• Picnicers and concertgoers. The catered picnic has always been a favorite of romantics; now, with the increasing popularity of outdoor symphony concerts, there is an additional demand for the elegant, moveable feast.

The possibilities are practically endless; the only limitations may be your own energy and imagination. Catering, with its low capital investment requirements, is one of the easiest businesses to get into, and chances are you'll have already acquired many of the necessary skills at home. The business is fast paced and exciting and, along with its monetary rewards, offers tremendous potential for creative fulfillment and just plain fun. If you have a knack for creating enticing edibles, if there is something special about your parties that others notice and appreciate, running your own catering business could be the dream come true: getting paid for doing what you love to do.

What It Takes

It goes without saying that a successful caterer must love working with food. Even those who hate to cook at home enjoy whipping up wonderfully creative party fare for their clients. And the food must not only taste delicious but also must look beautiful. "The hardest thing," says Kathie, "is that perfectionist part of it. It's something that has to look pretty, taste good — it has to be perfect.'' A caterer must also love to entertain. Her presence at the party must contribute to the festive atmosphere. "Anyone can make some hors d'oeuvres," says Peggy, "but it's the presentation and the service, the way the servers look, the way they react to the people at the party that's so important."

Like tastes in fashion, tastes in food change and as a professional caterer, you'll need to keep abreast of trends. For instance, Jane Wilson, of New York's "Party Box," notes that tastes are moving away from the heavier meat-based dishes and toward meals made with fruit, vegetables and grains. Not necessarily vegetarian, she says, just lighter. Jane also finds increasing numbers of customers opting for wine rather than hard liquor. How do you stay on top of such things? "In reading and listening and attending different parties, you find out what's hot and what's not," says Peggy Davenport. "This year duck was popular; last year it was pasta salad. Brie was really big two years ago." Peggy adds that using a variety of menus is important, especially if you're doing several parties each year for the same customer. "When you have one group of people that you're working with — we've done a lot of parties for the art museum — it inspires you to come up with new and different ideas. It keeps us more interested too, because after you've made 5,000 pieces of sesame chicken it's fun to do chicken paprikabobs for a change." Looking for and trying out new recipes can be one of the most exciting aspects of the business. "It's fun!" says Peggy. "Instead of getting into bed with *War and Peace*, I get into bed with *Bon Appetit!*"

Planning, caterers agree, is the key to any successful party. You can't be unorganized and hope to have a large, complex party come off well. "No way!" says Kathie. "It's even to the point that if you have a party on Saturday night, you get to sleep early on Friday night — you have to have all your senses together."

Occasionally, however, emergencies will come up no matter how well you've planned ahead. What if the deep fryer breaks down? Or an unexpected heat wave melts the salmon mousse? In situations like these, flexibility is the key. Peggy explains, "Let's say a mold doesn't mold right before the party. We don't go up to the client and say, 'Gee, you know that tomato aspic we were going to have? Well, let me tell you what happened!' They don't want to hear it. No excuses, no mistakes. If something does happen we just have to be creative enough and spontaneous enough to substitute something for it. It's like in a play when there are all kinds of little minor incidents going on that are mistakes, but they're covered up so well that nobody ever knows they're mistakes — just so you take care of it and don't make *your* problem *their* problem. That's part of the professionalism that's so important.''

The creative nature of the job notwithstanding, you'll need a certain amount of business sense. "The hardest part for me," says caterer Esther Cohen, "is getting myself to sit down and focus on the organizing and book work, the paperwork. I don't mind working a whole lot of hours, but sitting down and dealing with the dollars and cents of it is hard. I'll spend far too much time worrying about it rather than actually doing it."

What kind of social atmosphere prevails in your area? Are big, catered parties the rule, or do most people lean toward informal at-home get-togethers? A low-key social environment doesn't necessarily mean your catering business won't succeed, but it is an indication of the adjustments you'll need to make. What about your own social connections? Do you have friends who hire caterers? If so, their referrals could be an important source of business.

Start-up Costs and Expenses

Unlike many food businesses, catering is a low-investment venture, simply because the emphasis is on service. Many caterers have started with almost no capital and, by arranging to perform their services mostly on their customers' premises, have kept their operating costs to a minimum. Esther Cohen's one-woman catering service is a perfect example. Esther specializes in ethnic cuisine which she says is a hybrid of natural and gourmet foods. She goes to her customer's home, prepares the meal — generally Moroccan, Chinese, Japanese, or Indian cuisine — and then, with traditional dress, music and table settings, she brings the particular country's culture as well as its cuisine to the party. Her customers are enchanted. "I like to create environments — just bring the whole atmosphere into your home."

Esther started her catering business last year when a friend challenged her to make a certain amount of money in one month's time. She had always loved cooking for other people, and it occurred to her that she could do some parties. "Because I didn't have any capital to start this business, I've gotten a lot of the things I need through trading. I needed plates and bowls, so I've gone to different potters and told them what I was doing and asked them to do trades. They say they wish more people would think of this. I'll put a little card for their pottery on my table and maybe cook them a dinner."

Esther's parties generally range from about eight to a dozen people, although she says that by hiring extra help, she can accommodate as many as thirty. For larger groups, you'll find that much more advance preparation is required, and that means you'll need a work space of your own. Because of health codes, you probably won't be able to use your own kitchen, but that doesn't mean you have to invest $20,000-$30,000 in a new kitchen. There are several low-cost alternatives.

- You can convert your basement, garage or utility porch, using a second-hand restaurant stove and refrigerator. Even used cupboards, shelves and work tables can be found. Is there a bakery in your town that's going out of business? It's possible the owner would be happy to sell you his equipment at a bargain price.

- Churches, synagogues, schools and various types of clubs have kitchens that are seldom used. You might be able to rent space there.

- Sometimes you can rent part of a restaurant kitchen. Peggy and Kathie sublease space in a restaurant owned by friends. The restaurant serves only breakfast and lunch, so the two women can use the kitchen any time after 2 p.m. and on weekends.

Another big advantage to this arrangement is that Peggy and Kathie are able to use all the restaurant's cooking equipment. "We have had very little overhead," says Kathie. "We've just bought a few things ourselves: a couple of deep fryers, trays, baskets, uniforms."

• You'll need some equipment to take on the job, but for the most part, renting is more practical and often cheaper than buying. You avoid upkeep, repairs and storage problems along with the initial expense. "We get all our rentals from a rental company," says Peggy. "To buy all our own china and glassware and silverware and bring it to the kitchen and sterilize it to specifications is just a real pain in the neck."

• Check on insurance requirements; you may need special liability coverage.

It's the personal touch, the look and taste of quality food carefully prepared, that makes Secret Service Caterers so popular. "We make everything ourselves. We don't buy any frozen things and pass them on. And it really shows; you can tell the difference." If making things yourself means greater control of the quality, it also means a lot more work. Obviously, unless you plan to limit yourself to very small parties, you can't do everything yourself. One solution is to hire helpers, and contrary to the popular lament, good help is not that hard to find.

• Subcontract with your talented friends to make their specialties. For instance, you might know someone who's a whiz at homemade pasta or fresh fruit tarts. You can hire friends to act as waitresses and waiters, bartenders or dishwashers.

• Housewives and college students often welcome the opportunity to make extra money in a festive atmosphere.

What to Charge

If there is a money problem among caterers, it's the tendency to charge too little. Pricing your services is not an exact science; there are many variables to consider and finding the best pricing formula usually takes time and experience. "The two most important factors," explains Peggy, "are the number of people and the items being served. The more people there are at the party, the less per person we need to charge. If there are 200 people, we might charge $6 a person. But for 100 people, it would be $8 a person for the same meal."

The reason for the difference lies in the basic overhead required to set up any party, regardless of size. Up to a point, adding more people to the guest list just makes the labor more cost efficient. "Once you've got your momentum going," says Peggy, "it's easy just to keep going. I mean, as long as you're doing a hundred pieces of sesame chicken, why not do three hundred?"

Another influencing factor is the style of service, which may range from self-service, where the customer picks up pre-packaged meals and serves them herself, to full service, where virtually every detail of the party is handled by the caterer. A stand-up cocktail party for twenty-five, for example, might cost as little as $3.50 per person; fully staffed, the same party might cost $20 per person, and a full service dinner could run as high as $50 per person.

One rule of thumb is to charge triple the cost of the food, which works if you don't have to rent a lot of expensive equipment or pay many extra workers. And extras — such as fresh flowers — can really boost expenses.

Another method is to take all the expenses of the party — food, transportation, equipment costs, rental of linen and china, flowers, wages for helpers — figure out how many hours of your time will be invested in the party and how much you want to make per hour, add it all up and divide by the number of people at the party. Then submit your bid; chances are you'll be competing with at least one other caterer.

One advantage of catering over other food businesses is that it involves very little risk. Unlike a baker, for example, who delivers products and then waits thirty to sixty days for payment, caterers need never invest their own money. Instead, a deposit is obtained (usually 50 percent) to cover the costs of food and other expenses, and the balance is collected after the party.

There are several instances in which lowering your rates might be good strategy:

- It's helpful at first, while establishing your cashflow, to cultivate a base of regular customers. You might offer these "preferred customers" a reduced rate in exchange for repeat business you can count on.

- Consider the customer's budget. You might charge less for a family wedding dinner than you would for a corporate New Year's Eve bash.

- You might offer to cater a big charity benefit for less in order to make contacts and take advantage of the free advertising generally given such events.

Advertising

In the catering business, word of mouth will be your best form of advertising. In fact, personal referrals have brought Secret Service Caterers so much business that, except for passing out their business cards, Peggy and Kathie do no advertising. One happy result, they say, is that in four years of operation, they've had only one customer fail to pay — a good record for any business. "The clientele is pretty consistent," explains Kathie. "There's always a sense of knowing people so there's a little bit of trust there."

If you don't feel you want to depend on referrals alone, however, there are several low-cost options. Esther Cohen distributes fliers and posters. "I was a silkscreener so I can do all my own layout and lettering and print my own posters. It allows me to use all my talents and it's a lot cheaper."

Newspaper ads can be a good way of getting your name out quickly; most newspapers include a services directory in their classified ad section. And do explore sources of free publicity, such as newspaper human interest articles. One caterer drew loads of attention to her business when she engineered an "Ultimate Brownie Contest." The entries were judged by widely known members of the community and the event was written up in all the local papers.

Coping With the Pressure

"There's so many details. It's like being a waitress: you have four tables at a station and you can't remember who ordered what — it's sensory overload," says Kathie O'Donnell in describing the pressures of catering. Without question, it's a high-pressure kind of job, structured not unlike a Broadway play where each night there is a different audience and only one chance to get it right. No retakes. There are two basic reasons for the pressure: First, you work with perishables that can be ruined fairly easily; second, unless yours is a one-person operation, there are aspects of the work that are not within your control — and *that* can be maddening.

"You're so dependent on other people," says Peggy. "We make all the arrangements and if somebody doesn't come through, it's our reputation that's at stake.

Kathie continues, "Like for the tailgate picnic we did at the stadium, we had somebody contracted to make 100 blintzes for us and that morning he called and said, 'I've locked them in the kitchen and I can't find the key and so I'm sorry but . . .' He showed up ten minutes before the party."

"It's not so much what we do that I worry about," says Peggy, "but what other people are going to do or not do."

Long, Late Hours

Another thing to consider is that like virtually all the entertainment-related businesses, catering is somewhat seasonal, peaking during the November and December holidays. January traditionally has been the slowest month, with business picking up again for Valentine's and St. Patrick's Day parties. And you can count on working weekends, holidays and evenings, since the times everyone else parties will be your prime working hours. Keeping such a demanding schedule could be hard on a two-career family, that is, unless both parties are involved in the business. Coping, say Peggy and Kathie, is a matter of planning and consideration.

"It is hard," confesses Peggy. "I'm engaged and my fiance is very flexible in what he does and that's good. Many times I can't do things because of parties — I keep a calender on my refrigerator so he knows pretty much when I can't do something. You just have to be flexible and work around each other."

Since Kathie is married and has one child, scheduling time with her family is even more complicated. "I've blocked off the time because John, my husband, works a regular nine-to-five job and I make sure I've got everything done by the time he gets home so we can spend time together. I try to make it more of a job. But when the parties come, you're so stressed out that it's hard to relate to another person."

Many of the problems and pressures can be minimized by finding a compatible partner to share both the worries and the workload. Partners can take turns giving each other a break from what could otherwise become a 24-hour-a-day obsession. "When we get calls," says Peggy, "Kathie and I divide them. She'll handle a party for Tuesday and I'll handle a party for Friday night. So that gives us some relief. And you just divorce yourself when it's not your party — we don't check up on each other."

"It's like a marriage," says Kathie. "When one gets more up-tight, the other one stays calm. We don't usually lose it at the same time."

. . .And Many Satisfactions

For all its pressures and demands, catering can be one of the most exciting and profitable service businesses going. The payoffs run the gamut from creative and social outlets to freedom and independence to just plain good money per hour invested. For the person blessed with a gracious personality and culinary talents, it can be a labor of love, the chance to make money at a favorite pastime. One of the nicest benefits, say caterers, is the opportunity to meet interesting people in festive surroundings. "For me," says Esther Cohen, "it's being able to reach a lot of different kinds of people and talk to them and share myself with them. I feel like I'm giving them something special, an appreciation for food I feel isn't very common. I feel I can create a happy occasion for my customers — I can become friends with people."

Independence is another important attraction. To a certain extent, caterers must take advantage of work when it's available, but there is still freedom and flexibility built into the business. "I enjoy being able to go away for a little bit, not being tied down to something that's very structured," says Peggy. "And not having to answer to someone else is nice," adds Kathie. Both women strongly agree that they wouldn't go back to working in an office, even though catering means long hours on your feet all day. "I actually like the exertion," says Kathie, laughing. "At least you're getting exercise and burning calories while you're working. It's not like a desk job where you're always just sitting there."

Building a business of your own can bring a great sense of pride and accomplishment; for many people just seeing an idea transformed into reality is enormously satisfying. All things considered, say Peggy and Kathie, that sense of accomplishment has been the thing they've liked the most about their venture. "I think the most rewarding part of the job," says Kathie, "is that Peggy and I just talked about this as a lark and it's turned into a good, successful business."

Chapter 7
Publishing Services

If you're like most people, when you think of publishing you think of big business — something on the scale of *Better Homes and Gardens* or Random House, for example.

While it's true that publishing has historically involved big business, we are moving further into the information age and specialization is becoming increasingly important. In providing highly specialized information small, specialty publishers often have competitive advantages over the giants of publishing.

The experience of the huge circulation, mass market magazines such as *Look* and *Saturday Evening Post* offer an instructive example. For decades these general interest magazines flourished, taking on the status of American institutions. But in the late 60s and early 70s — just as we began to really enter the information age — people began to want more specialized information. The "something for everybody" approach began to lose favor, and the mass market magazines began to rapidly lose ground to an incredible array of special interest magazines covering everything from compost science to hang gliding to running. (Bob Anderson was 17 years old when he invested $100 and hand-folded and hand-stapled the first issue of the magazine he started for runners — a magazine that today is known as *Runners' World*).

The demand for specialized information continues to grow today, and new opportunities are constantly developing in specialized markets. Ours is a society of special interest groups, each one eager for the latest information, and just as the demand for new publications has never been greater, the obstacles to entering the publishing field have never been fewer. This chapter will examine three different types of publishing opportunities.

Newsletter Publishing

One of the ways in which this country's hunger for information has manifested itself is in the booming two-billion-dollar-a-year newsletter industry. There are wonderful success stories in the newsletter field, too:

- Milton Zelman's "Chocolate News" is a bimonthly newsletter printed on chocolate-scented paper. With some 18,000 chocoholic subscribers paying $9.95, Zelman grosses about $180,000 a year. In an article in *Money* magazine, Zelman says his overhead costs are "quite low."

- While still in his twenties, Mark Hulbert invested $5,000 to launch a newsletter that evaluates the recommendations and monitors the predictions of other newsletters in the investment field. His monthly "Hulbert Financial Digest" has about 5,000 subscribers paying $135 — almost $350,000 in annual gross revenues.

- Andrew Harper turned a love of travel into a tremendously lucrative career. His $45-a-year "Hideaway Report" keeps his 14,000 affluent subscribers informed about the very best hideaways — fabulous lodges, inns and hotels — around the globe.

There are currently thousands of subscription newsletters produced each month. Who's reading them? Who's publishing them? What is a newsletter anyway?

In the simplest terms, a newsletter is a kind of personalized information service, a specialized, in-depth report concentrating on a focused subject area of interest to a limited number of people — usually groups or organizations too small to support a magazine. Unlike general interest publications, a newsletter's main attraction is that it meets the demand for highly specialized information — "inside dope" — on a particular subject.

Can a Newsletter Really Make Money?

Anyone familiar with the mortality rate of magazines is probably wondering how anyone can expect to make money with a newsletter when so many magazines fail. The answer is that newsletters and magazines work on completely different operating principles, the chief distinction being their respective sources of revenue. The magazine publisher's biggest challenge lies in the fact that his major source of revenue comes from selling advertising space, which sounds simple but actually results in a kind of double bind that contributes to high overhead. High advertising rates can only be justified by large circulations, because advertisers naturally want their ads to reach the largest number of potential buyers possible. Since large circulation figures depend on low subscription rates, the publisher is forced to be even more dependent on advertising revenues, and this is where costs begin to soar. The best way of getting advertisers is through personal attention in terms of sales calls and general hand-holding. This kind of service takes a lot of time and the publisher's solution is to hire an ad representative whose sole job is to make sure the advertiser's needs are met. With every addition to the payroll, the publisher's overhead increases. Printing costs go up with the inclusion of expensive color photography and glossy production used to sell products. And with every increase in overhead there is a corresponding increase in risk.

Newsletter publishers, on the other hand, beat the built-in cost spiral by eliminating advertising, relying instead on higher subscription rates. But would a reader be willing to pay higher rates

— up to $2,000 a year — for an "information service"? He would if the newsletter contained vital information — no frills, no advertising, just the up-to-date inside track on what was happening in his field. Going back to the idea that knowledge is the new strategic resource, it's not surprising that businesses make up the largest segment of the newsletter market. Many business people believe a newsletter pays for itself by providing information they need to compete, to make decisions about where to invest and where to cut back. They find out which markets are hot and which are declining, and about new legislation that may affect their businesses. They may decide they can't afford *not* to subscribe if they think the competition may be subscribing. Besides, even with high rates, it still costs less to subscribe than it would to gather the information on their own. People in other fields agree. In addition to business subscribers, there are thousands of investors, collectors, hobbyists and professionals with similar needs for staying current in their fields of interest. The answer is yes, newsletters can and do make money.

How to Get Started

Choosing a subject is the obvious first step to entering the newsletter field.

- If you already have specialized knowledge in a given area, the trick will be to find a way to capitalize on it. Are you a whiz at the stock market? Do you have banking or real estate or health care market expertise? You'll have a head start if you select a subject that lies in your own field of experience, simply because you already have a feel for the kind of information that is needed by those in your field and you probably have some contacts or knowledge of where to find the information.

- Do you have a hobby shared by others who would appreciate trading ideas? Clem Labine and his wife received a real trial-and-error education when they set about remodeling their Victorian brownstone. The experience convinced Clem that other do-it-yourselfers, facing the same problems, would pay for ideas and advice in tackling their own restoration projects. Today his newsletter, "The Old House Journal," has about 75,000 subscribers and grosses around $900,000 annually.

• Could your special insight into a particular problem help others? When Dennis Dunn discovered that his infant son had a learning disability, he started a monthly newsletter called "Growing Child." The publication offers advice on childhood development to about 275,000 subscribers, netting Dunn a yearly profit of around $100,000.

Narrow Your Focus

The biggest mistake beginners make, say newsletter publishers, is trying to cover too broad a subject. Their advice is, the narrower your focus, the more detailed and specific you can be and the more valuable that information will be to your reader. Granted, not everyone will be able to use such narrowly focused information, but the ones who can will gladly pay more for it.

Check the Competition

Ideally, your chosen field would have no other newsletters (or at least no other newsletters that could match the quality of your editorial content). To see if your idea has already been taken, you can consult the Oxbridge Directory of Newsletters or the National Directory of Investment Newsletters, both available at many libraries.

Putting Your Newsletter Together

To attract subscribers, your newsletter must be timely and authoritative. Again, editorial content — not fancy or expensive layout — is the most important factor. Members of the garden club might enjoy poems, humorous anecdotes and witty editorializing, but business people and serious hobbyists — the ones willing to pay premium prices — want facts.

- Newsletters are brief, generally between two and eight pages.

- Use short pages with wide margins. Two-column formats, especially for the front page, are popular.

- Writing should be direct, to the point.

- Layout, design and typography should be simple and consistent. One mistake novices make is to use too many type styles and layout variations. A logo and layout that are fairly consistent from issue to issue will make your newsletter more easily recognizable. Many publishers believe front-page articles should be ended on the front page; it's irritating to the reader, they feel, to have to keep turning pages in order to finish an article. If you must "jump" a story to another page, the back page is a good place to do it. The reader can simply turn over the issue to finish reading the story, then turn it over again to get back to other important material. (It's logical and a standard practice to position your most newsworthy material in the front.)

- A calendar of events can be a great draw. People will subscribe just to find out about upcoming conventions, trade shows, seminars and meetings.

How to Get Subscribers

Most newsletter publishers spend less than 10 percent of their operating budgets on advertising to sell subscriptions. This encouraging fact is basically due to the nature of the newsletter medium; if you've chosen your subject carefully, selling subscriptions won't be so much a matter of competing with other newsletters and magazines as finding ways of reaching people in your target group. Names of potential subscribers may be available from a number of diverse sources.

- Cultivate a mailing list of names from trade association directories, conference registers and other newsletters.

- Many organizations will provide lists of members if your newsletter contains information which could be helpful to them.

- "Direct Mail List Rates and Data" is a guide to mailing lists that you can rent. Rental rates are usually less than $100 per thousand names.

- You can place small ads in trade journals or special interest magazines. Andrew Harper used this approach — placing modest but effective ads in publications like the *Wall Street Journal* — to build his subscriber list for the "Hideaway Report."

Setting a Subscription Price

In order for your newsletter to turn a profit, you'll need to set a subscription price that will cover, in addition to printing and postage costs, your time for research, writing and promotion. After your costs are met, price becomes a matter of what the market will bear. While some newsletters that are primarily published to promote other businesses sell for as little as $5 a year, others go for as much as $2,000, depending on how valuable the information is to the subscriber.

One tip: Since printing and postage will major be expenses, you might find it more profitable to limit your circulation (by tailoring your information to a narrow, specialized audience) and charge a higher rate.

Business Directories

Maureen Regan and Brenda Exline stand to make a significant profit this year. The two women, borrowing an idea that's caught on in several major cities, will publish "The Women's Yellow Pages," a directory of businesses in their city that are owned and operated by women. The response has been phenomenal: fifteen salespeople are busy taking ads for the directory while a phone operator is kept practically breathless answering calls from people requesting copies. A popular local bookstore will carry the directory at $5 per copy, and if only half the planned printing of 20,000 sell, Maureen and Brenda will gross over $50,000 — not counting revenues from the advertisers. That's not bad for four months work.

Why would any business owner, male or female, choose to advertise in a local directory when other media — TV, radio, newspapers, telephone yellow pages — reach so many more people? The answer, of course, is cost; traditional forms of advertising can be extremely expensive. It goes almost without saying that television and radio advertising are beyond the reach of many, many small businesses, and as costs continue to rise, even the more economical media like newspaper and telephone directory ads can quickly strain advertising budgets. Direct mail can be very effective, but with the costs of mailing lists, printing and postage, it could cost a business owner $5,000 or more to reach 25,000 people. Word-of-mouth advertising, naturally, costs nothing, but results are generally slow in coming and sporadic; you tend to get too much business when you don't need it and not enough when you do. An increasingly popular alternative for cost-conscious businesses — especially low budget home businesses — is advertising in business directories.

Is the demand for directories great enough to support a business in your area? That depends on a number of factors, but on the whole, the evidence is very positive.

- We live in an age of growing self-employment. Over 60,000 new businesses are launched each year, and their numbers alone make a substantial market for the directory publisher.

- There are more than 5 million home-based businesses in the U.S. today; many experts believe that number will double over the next decade. These budget-minded people will need less expensive ways of reaching their customers than many of the traditional advertising media permit.

- Our culture is characterized by rapid change and innovation. More than ever, business people are open to new ways of marketing, including new methods of advertising.

Directory publishing requires minimal capital to get started, and all things considered, it promises to be a very good full- or part-time business opportunity.

Getting Started

The first step is to analyze your market. Does your town have enough potential advertisers to support a directory? If not, you can expand your geographical coverage to take in two or three small towns or perhaps your whole county or region. Since the ideal population for a directory is between 35,000 and 100,000, many cities will be too large for a single directory. In that case, you might divide your area into two or more sections, using a major street as a boundary line.

Does your town have a central business district? If so, you might want to publish a directory especially for those merchants. Leslie Goodwin produced a map and directory specifically designed to draw traffic into the downtown mall area of her town. Finding advertisers was fairly simple, says Leslie. By walking through the area, hitting every single business, she was able to sell 150 ads.

For larger areas, however, calling on potential customers in person would probably not be practical. Instead, you'll want to telephone them, which will require compiling a list of leads. Businesses which are not currently listed in the telephone directory may be your best potential customers, but how can you find out about them? You can start by writing down the names of everyone you know who has a small business. Ask friends to help you, and go over the services listings in your local papers. Check the bulletin boards in grocery and hardware stores for business cards. Bulletin boards in local music stores might display ads for piano tuning and guitar lessons. Every time you talk to a prospect, ask them who they know who might be interested in being listed. Don't throw away your list; you'll want to update it and you'll need it for your next issue.

One caution: Before you start selling ad space, make sure you know what the job will entail from start to finish and know for sure that you *can* finish. If for any reason you aren't able to fulfill your commitment of coming out with the directory, you'll have to refund all the money you've collected. In any case, it would be wise to set aside 60 percent of your ad revenues to cover printing costs.

What to Charge

Because there are so many variables in producing a directory, it would be really helpful to get advice from someone who's already published one, preferably in a nearby community. Even so, says Leslie Goodwin, it would be difficult to cite a set formula. "So much depends on how many advertising spaces there are. You have to sit down and figure out what it's going to cost to produce, how much money you want to make for yourself, and how much you can charge and still be competitive. A lot depends on what kind of production you're going to do; the printing costs can vary as much as $5,000."

As important as it is to cover your costs, it's doubly important that you reduce your costs any way you can without compromising essential quality. "There is so much detail in this kind of publishing venture and that costs money," says Leslie. "A directory was good for me because I had done production for a 60-page magazine and had all the skills. I knew how to sell, how to compose ads. I knew how to get the best deals from the printers and how to provide the materials for the printer so it would cost the least." If you don't have a background in journalism or advertising, it may be worth-while to find a partner who can help with some judicious cost cutting. Meanwhile, here are some ideas you can use as a starting point.

- One way of simplifying things is to use a format similar to a classified ad. This way, you can charge a flat rate for, say, six lines then add one or two extra lines at $5 a line. This format also makes layout and alphabetizing easier. Typeset material looks more professional than typewritten copy, but it also costs more.

- Leslie charged her advertisers $40 for a 10-line listing. In some cases, for an extra charge, she also designed ads for customers. As an added selling point, she gave her designs to her customers, who could use them any way they wanted.

- Ad rates for the Women's Yellow Pages range from $95 for a standard listing in one of 250 categories to $375 for a full-page ad.

- Rates can be based on the size of the market, i.e., $35 for smaller communities of 75,000 or fewer; $45 for cities of 75,000 or more.

- You might want to offer discounts to businesses who place ads in more than one category: for example, $40 for the first ad, $32.50 for the second, and so on.

- Leslie says she learned the hard way never to do a bid for a merchants association without having them pay for the bid. "I did about two week's work on a bid for [one merchants association] and they took all the information and did it themselves. They used the same map style, the same type style, even some of the ads I had produced. It was copied right down to the last detail. I had given them tips on the basis that I was going to do the job, and I never got anything out of it.''

Early spring and fall are agreed to be the best times to publish directories. Since it takes about three months to gather ads and one month to have the printing done, you should start about four months in advance. Do you want to publish once or twice a year? A large community could see sufficient growth to justify two printings which would mean more profits for you.

Distribution

No matter how inexpensive an advertising medium is, it's no bargain if it doesn't bring business to the advertiser. The key to making that happen — and to ensuring a high number of repeat customers for your next printing — is effective distribution. In fact, says Leslie, ''Distribution is ninety percent of it. If I publish the directories but don't put them in places where they can be picked up, it's the same as not doing anything at all.''

You can start by sending a copy of your directory to each advertiser; if he has space to display them, he might want to keep several dozen to give away. The next step would be to go to area businesses such as real estate offices, banks, restaurants and hardware stores and ask if they'd like to have a hundred copies to distribute. ''I took them to the Chamber of Commerce,'' says Leslie, ''and to hotels and information centers — any place that had a good influx of tourists. People really appreciated that. Sometimes people who had relatives coming into town would want to get maps for them, so I'd ship them the maps. The more you get distributed, the better.''

The Importance of Attitude

"If you have any self-doubts when you go in to sell advertising, it shows all over your face like you're wearing a poster."

Leslie Goodwin

Advertising sales, explains Leslie, is like no other kind of selling. By comparison, the retailer's job is easy. His customer can hold the sweater in her hands, try it on, and when she lays down her $35, she knows exactly what it is she's bought. Advertising, on the other hand, is the most nebulous of services; what you sell is completely intangible. Unlike the woman who leaves the store with her sweater, your customer has no guarantee his ad in your directory will bring the results he wants. Ultimately, selling the ad will depend on his faith in your ability to represent him well and, Leslie stresses, his chief cues will be your attitudes toward yourself and your work. "I'm a real firm believer in positivism. A positive attitude is something that will give anyone an edge in competing. The minute you think anything negative about the people you're selling to, or about your project or about yourself, then the other person has an advantage over you. You have to stay up."

Book Publishing

If you've ever dreamed of the glamour and excitement of the book publishing world but discounted it as a serious option because 1) you don't relish a corporate working environment and 2) you don't want to live in New York City, now is the time to take a second look at the possibilities.

You'll find that the same trends that have opened up ancillary fields have had just as profound an effect on publishing. For one thing, the industry has decentralized; New York is no longer considered the only acceptable location for book publishers. Even more encouraging is the shift away from bigness. At a time when major houses are selling out to conglomerates, small publishers are flourishing.

Trends Creating the Opportunities

Many small publishers are actually self-publishers — writers and editors who have found commercial publishing to be too restrictive for their tastes. Rather than have the editorial content of their works dictated by commercial imperative, they've opted to skip the depressing rounds of submission and rejection and simply publish their work themselves. If it came to it, some would work for nothing — wearing the hats of writer, editor, designer, typesetter and secretary — in order to see a cherished work published. Increasingly that sacrifice is not necessary, and it's mainly because of three factors:

- *The Nation-wide Trend Toward Self-sufficiency*

    In a movement that began in the 60s, a generation of baby boomers has shunned big business and mass production, choosing instead to remodel their own homes, plant their own gardens and fix their own bicycles. One result has been tremendous growth in the market for non-fiction how-to books.

    Because the large New York publishers were slow to recognize this trend as something more than a passing fad — and because the fiscal character of large-scale publishing doesn't encourage speculation in small new markets — small publishers around the country were able to capitalize on this growing how-to book market and gain a foothold for expanding into other types of books. A big company with a correspondingly big overhead can't afford to risk investing in a vegetarian cookbook that might sell only a few thousand copies. Its management looks instead for the commercial hits, the blockbusters, leaving the rest of the field more or less open for the small publisher who, with a streamlined operation, can often make money on sales of as few as two or three thousand copies of a book.

- *Technical Advancements*

    The advent of word processing, phototypesetting, and offset printing has made the book production process much less expensive than it was just a few years ago. It no longer requires massive amounts of capital to get a modestly packaged book into print, and small publishers can gain just as much as the largest publishers by using the new technology. The technology is changing so fast that the greater flexibility of the small publishers may actually make it easier for them to keep up.

* *Widespread Acceptance of Paperbacks*
    Most small publishers have chosen to concentrate their efforts on quality paperback books, which are much cheaper to produce than hardbound books. At the same time, budget-minded consumers are increasingly willing to forego hardcover packaging in exchange for big savings.

Potential for Growth

The distinctions between small publishing and large-scale publishing are not always clear, and there is always the potential for a small press book to cross over into the commercial mainstream. The publishers of books like *Laurel's Kitchen, Anybody's Bike Book* and *The Whole Earth Catalog* can attest that, when such a crossover occurs, it's a happy event for all concerned. About 10 percent of the titles on bestseller lists, in fact, now come from small publishers.

Book Packaging

Book packaging, or producing, is a relatively new type of opportunity in the book publishing field. A book packager is a person who comes up with ideas and coordinates the writing and development of the resulting books, usually working with a network of freelance writers, editors and designers in the process. At some point in the development of the packaged book — and that point may vary considerably — the work is sold to a commercial publisher or other source for distribution.

Although small publishers sometimes begin operations with extremely limited capital, book packagers can go into business with even less of an investment. If you can dream up a really good book idea and know a writer who could do a good job with the book, you may be able to get an established publisher to advance you the money to develop the book so that no investment whatsoever would be required on your part.

Suppose, for example, that you come up with an idea for a book that offers information on a new, easier way to learn computer programming. What's more, you know a freelance writer in your city who specializes in computer books but who is currently between projects and looking for work. You are confident that you can do a good job of editing the manuscript once it is written, so you decide to approach several publishers that would be likely to show an interest in the book.

As luck would have it, the first publishers you talk to are immediately interested in your idea. They offer you an $8,000 advance and a 7.5 percent royalty on each book sold. The contract stipulates that your completed manuscript must be satisfactory to the publisher or else you must return the advance.

You agree to their terms and go to talk to your writer friend. There are basically two ways you can contract with him — either on a flat-fee, work-for-hire basis, or on a royalty basis. With a flat-fee arrangement you agree to pay your friend a given amount — say $5,000 — to write the book, and no royalties are involved. With a royalty arrangement you might agree to pay your friend an advance of only $1,000, but you also agree to share some part of any future royalty payments with him.

Would the above scenario be a smart business deal for all concerned? If the book idea really is a good one, and both the writer and publisher do their jobs well, it could very well be.

Book packaging is steadily growing in popularity. The large New York publishers are well aware that they are not always able to move as quickly as small publishers to tap new ideas and new markets, and they feel that working with packagers is one way to compensate. Working with packagers also allows publishers to increase the number of new books they publish without increasing the size of their staffs. It's not unusual for editors with the large publishing houses to turn to packagers for help in developing their own ideas for new books, and in some cases editors are recommending that authors work through packagers rather than working directly with the publisher.

Bill Adler, a packager who has worked on best-sellers such as *The I Love New York Diet,* predicts continued growth in this area. He was quoted in *Publishers Weekly* saying that within five years "more than 25 percent of the nonfiction trade books published in this country will be packaged books. Publishers," he continued, "are beginning to recognize that there are distinct advantages in having creative professionals deliver completed manuscripts that can be published with minimum editorial involvement and cost by the publisher."

Creative individuals who have good book ideas but who lack the capital or the inclination to form a publishing company are also well served by the packaging approach. If you are interested in pursuing the opportunities in this field, you should realize, however, that until you have established a reputation for producing high quality, salable books, your stock in trade will be ideas. That means your proposals to publishers will be all-important. They must be enticing yet accurate descriptions of the book. Your cost estimates will have to be on target, because once you've negotiated a contract it's very unlikely you'll be able to go back and negotiate an increase.

Exciting Prospects

If you've been storing up reams of manuscripts or stacks of research files, now is the time to unpack them. Opportunities for combining your writing, editorial and business skills have never been more plentiful. In publishing, as in so many other services, you can work at home — and your home can be just about anywhere. You can devise your own schedule, too, for publishing can be a profitable weekend diversion or a passion that consumes all your waking hours; you can work as much or as little as your interests and standard of living dictate.

Perhaps even more important, in the publishing field you can determine your own direction. Ours is such a manifold culture that no matter what your journalistic bent, with the right approach you're almost certain to find an audience. Whether your communication is directed to business people or farmers, to antique collectors or boating enthusiasts, there is something consummately rewarding about seeing your ideas — or the ideas of someone you respect — take shape on the printed page.

You're in the right place at the right time to consider self-employment in publishing. You couldn't ask for a more fertile marketplace for your abilities than our information-hungry society.

Chapter 8
Image Consulting

Virginia is about to make a career change. After ten years of teaching junior high school math, she has decided to enter the highly competitive computer sales market. Suddenly her old wardrobe standbys, the comfortable polyester slacks and turtlenecks, don't seem quite appropriate anymore. What she needs now is a more polished look, one that will communicate authority and professionalism.

At forty, Gordon is part of a new breed of family physicians. In establishing his own practice, he wants to foster a team approach to health care and a more informal relationship with his patients. He's decided to abandon some of the austere medical office trappings in favor of a warmer, more personal atmosphere. A great place to start, he feels, is his own image. He'd like to find a way of dressing that would instill confidence in others without intimidating them.

Ruth, recently widowed at fifty-five, believes that age is less a matter of years than a state of mind and body. After a year of faithful exercise and healthful eating, she's never felt better, more alive — and it shows. Now it's time to whip her wardrobe and makeup into shape.

Virginia, Gordon and Ruth are representative of the untold thousands who have come to realize the importance that appearance plays in the way they feel and perform. Throughout our culture, there is a growing awareness of the profound impact ones' image can make on confidence and self-esteem, personal relationships — and career achievements. And as people become more aware, they're doing something about it. More and more frequently, retailers see customers shopping with small, plastic-encased color charts in hand, looking for clothes with "congenial" colors. Nowadays, makeup consultants often have clients ask whether a certain eyeshadow is right for a "Fall" or "Summer" type. Everyone, it seems, has "had their colors done" at least once. Why this new interest in being "pulled together"?

In part, this trend can be seen as one more product of a decade-long quest for physical and emotional excellence which is most noticeable among — but certainly not exclusive to — a generation of baby boomers now coming into their own. As one image consultant has observed, "A lot of people come to us as they're completing an inner growth, and the color analysis and fashion typing are just the outward signs of the growth."

Appearance and Competitive Advantage

There is also a growing realization that outward appearance makes a difference not only in the ways we see ourselves, but also in the ways we're perceived and treated by others. No longer is the issue of public image important only for media types, entertainers and politicians. Now, secretaries and salespeople, bankers and dentists are also being enlightened about the ways a favorable image can translate to bottom-line results.

In the process of researching their book, *The Extra Edge: Success Strategies for Women*, Charlene Mitchell and Thomas Burdick asked female graduates of the Harvard Business School how important image had been in their career success to that point. Seventy-five percent of the women replied that image had been important or very important.

Perhaps even more impressive, a study reported by Nancy Josephson in *American Health* magazine has shown that appropriately flattering makeup and hairstyle not only make women look more employable, but also can get them higher salaries. Two hundred male and female interviewers were asked to rate the marketability of eight women, using only resumes and pictures of the women taken before and after beauty makeovers. Invariably, wrote Josephson, the women in the "after" photos were assigned better jobs and higher salaries — as much as 20 percent higher.

Obviously, the differences in the interviewers' assessments were based solely on appearance (after all, the resumes hadn't changed). What did the more polished "after" images say about the applicants that the "before's" didn't? One message conveyed is the value the woman puts on herself; messy hair or too much makeup, for instance, can communicate a lack of self-respect. On the other hand, a sleek, refined image suggests confidence and professionalism.

It's not surprising, then, that even in a tight economy, image-consulting businesses are flourishing. Actually, their customers believe that in a tough job market the competitive edge of a strong professional image is more important than ever.

High-Context Society vs. Low-Context Society

Still another factor in the trend toward image consciousness has to do with the high marks given in our culture for individuality; in our society, the object is not to blend in but to distinguish oneself. Judy Ruckstuhl, a consultant for "Color Profiles," explains this concept by contrasting attitudes toward image in a "high-context" society with those in a "low-context" society. In a high-context society (Saudi Arabia, for example) the idea is to dress so as to be identified as a member of a certain class. The American equivalent, Judy suggests, is the "fashion victim" who wears whatever is in vogue this season, regardless of whether it suits her. "The statement they strive to make, says Judy, "is, 'My husband can afford to dress me in the latest styles.' " In general, though, our society places a much higher value on individuality than is true of high-context societies. Here, the goal of fashion statements is to let the total image express the nuances of personality and lifestyle.

This creates more freedom, of course, but along with increased freedom comes more room for confusion and mistakes. Dressing to make a particular statement about oneself is a much more complicated task than merely "putting on the uniform," whether the uniform consists of the college student's jeans and Nike's, or the banker's three-piece navy pinstripe. It's one thing for a man to know what kind of image he wants to project, quite another to identify the colors and styles that make that particular fashion statement. It's not hard for a woman to recognize that someone else has the look she wants, but to translate that look into the clothes, makeup and hairstyle that are right for *her* can be challenging.

"Pacman and Kentucky Fried Chicken"

How well does the average consumer handle the problem of finding what best suits him or her among the virtually endless array of choices? "Every client we see," says Judy, "has a handle on one or two factors, but misses others, usually colors. Unfortunately, people don't necessarily gravitate toward their best colors. Part of the problem is that, unlike Eskimo kids who are taught to recognize twenty-three kinds of snow, we're not trained to distinguish subtle variations. Let's face it, in our culture, we're exposed to blatant neon colors — Pacman and Kentucky Fried Chicken — not suble gradations." The point is, why put up with questionable color choices when reliable guidance is available?

"Why indeed?" say thousands of people from all walks of life in all parts of the country. As a result, image consulting businesses are experiencing impressive growth.

The Image Consultant: . . .As Others See Us

What is it, exactly, that image consultants do? What enables them to transform the pleasant but average-looking woman into a classy vision of style and pizzazz? How do they go about teaching the conservative — even timid-looking — man to project boldness and authority? Three artistic and psychological principles are involved.

First, there is the concept of color analysis, based on the idea that because of the tones that naturally exist in a person's skin, hair and eye colors, he or she will look best in hues belonging to "congenial" color families. With a trained eye, the consultant can help the client identify those colors.

The second part of the process has to do with choosing the clothing styles that most flatter the client's figure. In order to do this, the consultant would consider such variables as height, weight and proportion.

The third and most subjective area would be determining what sort of image the individual wants to project. Usually, there is something that clients want to say about themselves in order to make the best first impression or to give themselves an edge over others; often, the effort is aimed at career success. The consultant's job, in this case, is to pull together all the right components — the colors, styles, makeup, hairstyle, maybe even posture and speaking voice — and put them together into one harmonious image that speaks for the client.

In addition to the color analysis and fashion typing that are basic to image consulting services, clients may opt for help with buying and coordinating their wardrobes. The consultant might visit the client's home, go through the closet and help separate usable items from the dead wood. By updating with accessories, a consultant can show clients how to get extra mileage from clothes that are in good condition but slightly past their fashion prime.

Many people, but especially men, feel overwhelmed by the vast selection of styles and colors available in department stores. They are easy prey for salespeople who sometimes are more interested in making a sale than in really helping the customer. Consultants can go shopping with their clients, teach them how to use their color charts to find the right clothing, and help them steer clear of styles that aren't appropriate for their particular image. They may also pass along tips for bargain hunting at sales and discount houses.

Immediate and Long-Range Benefits

A prospective client might wonder, "Sure, it would be fun to have an expert focus on me for two or three hours, and the little packet of colors may be handy, but what will it do for me in the long run? Here are some of the benefits consultants mention to their clients:

- You will save time and money. As a better informed, more competent shopper, you need never again squander your fashion dollars on clothes you won't like after wearing only a few times.

- You will see how to build a whole wardrobe of clothes and accessories that work together. You'll learn what you can do with gifts.

- You'll have that relaxed sense of confidence and self-esteem that comes from knowing you look the very best you possibly can.

The above describes, in a general way, some of the services image consultants offer their clients. The ways in which you translate these generalities into the specifics of your own business will depend on the color/fashion system you adopt for your own consulting philosophy. The important thing is that you believe wholeheartedly in what you're doing.

Debra Lindquist, "Color Profiles"

Debra Lindquist is, in the best sense, a walking advertisement for her image consulting firm, "Color Profiles." Tall and statuesque, she wears stylish clothes and her artfully applied makeup has been chosen to complement her natural coloring. In a vibrant alto voice, she speaks enthusiastically about her successful company.

"I really feel that people need a total concept. My business started out primarily as a personal color service; I truly feel that color is one aspect of image, but that it is only one. You can wear the right colors but if you have the wrong hairstyle, the wrong makeup or the wrong clothing styles, wearing the right colors isn't going to help you that much. So I see it as an integral part of the total picture. Now we actively teach courses in makeup, hair, figure, all of those things, as well as courses in how to shop. These are all extended services I feel the woman and the gentleman of the '80s are looking for.''

Do men really care about such things? One well known image consultant has said that the single biggest new market for consulting is the baby boom men now approaching 40 and getting into career positions where the right image can provide the cutting edge that wins promotion.

"About one-third of our customers are men, says Debra. I do feel that that age range is one where men are trying to make great strides in their careers, and it's okay now for them to seek services that, in the past, might have been more in the vanity field for women. Like when you go to beauty salons there might be men getting a perm along with the women, having facials, feeling that it's okay to think about skin care. I think just as women are out there striving to raise their level of credibility with image, men are out there too. So that's a definite market.''

The color system Debra and her consultants use is one she created herself. She explains that Color Profiles is not a "seasonal" system. She uses some 1,500 colors to compose a "body portrait" for each client, that is, a group of colors that match the tones found in the hair, skin and eyes of the person. Once the body portrait has been established, the client is assigned a fashion type and instructed in "classic styling." Debra's method, while perhaps more complicated and expensive than some others, has proved to be very popular. The company currently has some three dozen independent consultants based in cities from Sunnyvale, California to Geneva, Switzerland.

Background Requirements

"When I started doing color analysis ten years ago," says

Debra, "there were no people around for training classes, no people teaching this kind of information in college." Even now, writes Joan Timberlake in her book *Image Consulting, The New Career*, "there is no single background from which image consultants emerge." There are, however, certain kinds of work and academic experience that help supply the necessary skills. Debra Lindquist's education, a home economics degree with a minor in art, had given her a solid theoretical background from which to start. All that remained was to put theory into practice. "I've done a lot of teaching, I've worked in retail and direct sales, so I had a lot of experiences that led me to develop the concepts of this business. Then starting the business, finding that it was successful and going to work with literally thousands of clients reinforced some of my ideas because I had the 'laboratory experience' of actually seeing them work."

Image consulting requires a mixture of business and artistic skills. You can get an idea of where you stand by asking yourself a few questions:

1. *How well developed is my artistic perception?*

   In order to advise others, a consultant needs not only an eye for color, but also a sense of appropriateness and an understanding of artistic principles such as line and proportion. Art or design classes can help improve your visual acuity.

2. *How well developed is my knowledge of fashion? Do I enjoy working with clothing?*

   One of the best ways of gaining experience with fashion is to take a part-time job in one of the better retail stores in your area. There you can get on-the-job practice in working with different figure types and in advising customers about the styles which will work best for them.

3. *Do I truly enjoy working with people on a close, one-to-one basis?*

   "I'd say being people-oriented is very important,"

says Debra. "You have to sincerely enjoy working with people and want to help them. Some people are very good at putting themselves together but they couldn't care less about the rest of the population. They have to be able to visualize how someone could look. If they see a person who is maybe just a rather ordinary, non-plus person, they have to be able to . . . visualize what this person could be, how this person could look.

"We don't rule out anyone. We'll work with whatever it is you've got. We try not to let obstacles like age or weight keep us from acheiving our goals of helping someone look better."

4. *Do I tend to have confidence in my own judgment?*

Occasionally, you might suggest something for your client that, at first, is uncomfortable, just because it's new or different. It's important that you not let this hurt your feelings or shake your self-confidence. It's not uncommon for a woman to reject a new makeup look when it's first presented to her, for example, only to grow to love it once she's had time to adjust the way she sees herself.

"Sometimes you have to see where a person is coming from," explains Debra. "I don't think you can take a person from A to Z all in one leap. You may have to take them from A to E, and then when you get them to E, take them from E to R, and then from R to Z. That way it's a pleasant transition rather than a shock."

5. *How would I rate my public speaking skills?*

"Not only is it a competitive market for [business] people, it is also a competitive market for image consultants," Debra warns. "If you are a wonderful consultant but you can't convey to the public just how wonderful you are, no one will know about you or take advantage of your services." In other words, you'll need the ability to market yourself each time you're in the public eye. In addition to private consultations, you'll probably find yourself doing seminars and group consultations. You may be able to acquire the necessary confidence and polish by taking a public speaking course or by volunteering your services as a speaker or teacher for a church or community group.

6. *Can I work with people who don't fit into my own image preferences?*

Debra feels it's important to be able to work with all types, rather than only tall, willowy models. "Some people who are, for instance, very dark and dramatic often prefer to work with clients who are more like themselves, and they don't relate well to a lot of other people. I try to detach from the kinds of things I might wear and not consider those things when I'm working with a client."

The tendency to try to clothe the world in what is personally appealing can be a real problem for retailers who must sell to a broad range of people. Debra notes that you can often look at a store (especially a smaller store where the manager also does the buying) and then look at the manager and see that her store merchandise is an extension of her own closet. This actually presents a business opportunity for the alert image consultant, who can provide ideas for merchandising to a wider variety of customers.

7. *Do I have a positive outlook?*

A bouyant, optimistic attitude is essential in a high-touch field like image consulting. More than you know, your moods will affect your clients either positively or negatively. You can instill them with enthusiasm and confidence, or cause them to be more fearful, less ready to try new things, and ultimately, less likely to use your service again. That being the case, you must find ways of keeping your own attitudinal juices flowing.

The problem is compounded because running your own business can be an exhausting ongoing responsibility (although it is often fun and exciting, too). "When you are a captive from nine to five," Debra says, "well, you're a captive from nine to five, but the rest of your life is yours.

But when you are an entrepreneur, it's like being a homemaker; the work is never totally done. There is always one more thing you'd like to do. Something you just come to grips with is that you aren't ever going to get it all done; there'll always be one more thing, something you wish you could have done better. But that's just the way it is, so you don't beat your head against the wall.''

How can you avoid burning out? "I try to balance work with fun, pleasurable things that I feel are refreshing me, giving me new input on what I'm doing. I try to stop and look outside, smell the flowers now and then, so that I'm not just on a treadmill.''

8. *What about my own image?*

In a very real sense, as an image consultant you will be your own best advertisement for your business. Take a good look at yourself. If you can't be objective, get another consultant's input. Do you need to spiff up your wardrobe? Get a more current hairstyle? Trim a few pounds?

"I try to be 'put together' wherever I am," says Debra, "whether I'm at Safeway or a soccer game, because I feel that if people can't apply the knowledge that supposedly they're teaching, it reduces credibility.''

Getting Started

Once you've decided that image consulting is for you and you've found the right color system, your next step will be to get the specific training you need. The cost and amount of study required will depend on which kind of training program you choose. If your background has already provided you with most of the skills you'll need, you can simply fill in the gaps with a few low-cost or free classes at your local college. Most adult education programs offer courses in art or textiles, as well as business management. Many private business schools offer one- to two-year programs in fashion merchandising.

If you'll be starting more or less from scratch, however, it might be worth the investment to train with an established consulting business, for which you can expect to pay several hundred to several thousand dollars. The Color Profiles program includes "a beast" of a training period, all the necessary materials, use of the company name and help with setting up your own business. The cost is $3,000.

You will also need retail or direct sales experience. Many retail lines offer on-the-job training. Clinique cosmetics, for example, offers its in-store consultants an excellent series of workshops that include skin care and makeup techniques as well as sales tips on how to cultivate repeat customers and how to sell to a customer's individual needs. Avon, Amway, Mary Kay, Shaklee and many other direct sales companies provide products and training along with the chance to get your feet wet selling in a relaxed environment such as your own or your friends' homes. Working for someone else lets you learn without investing much of your own money.

A word of caution: You may see classified ads that read "MAKE $1,000 PER WEEK! Attractive, enthusiastic women needed for growing company. No experience necessary. P.O. Box -----" Some of these ads may be legitimate, but others are strictly cons. Don't send any money until you have a chance to investigate the company and make sure it will deliver what it promises.

At this point you can breathe a sigh of relief: Training will probably be your biggest expense. Now, on to setting up your office.

The Home Office

Naturally you'll want to keep your operating costs to a minimum, and working from your own home is one of the best ways to cut costs. But before you start bringing clients to your home, you'd better take a look at what that might — or might not — do for your own image. To represent you well, your home must not only be practical and comfortable, but must also provide a professional atmosphere. These are some points to consider:

   • Are you centrally located, easy to find? Is there adequate parking?

- You'll need a suitable place to meet with clients, one or two rooms that are fairly isolated from family noise and traffic. A bathroom set aside just for clients would be ideal.

- Will there be adequate phone coverage? Debra Lindquist, who started her business from her home, warns that "if children are answering the phone or if no one is answering the phone, it can ruin your business." An answering service might be well worth the cost.

- You'll need one white-walled room, preferably with both natural and incandescent or "full-spectrum" flourescent lighting. Ordinary flourescent lights tend to give people an unflattering chartreuse cast.

Materials and Equipment

- If your training program doesn't provide materials, you'll need to buy either fabric drapes or swatches. (Try to use good sized swatches instead of stingy little clippings.) You might also want to use displays with color photos of male and female models who typify the various color or fashion types.

- Business cards and stationery are part of your professional image; you might also want to have brochures printed.

- Videotaping equipment can help you compete in the image consulting arena, and fortunately, costs are coming down.

Continuing Education

Few fields are so characterized by change as fashion; you'll want to keep yourself abreast of all new trends. Most consultants subscribe to several trade publications (such as *Women's Wear*

Daily), as well as the major fashion magazines. And don't forget the dozen or so good books on makeup techniques by well known artists.

What to Charge

Fees vary with the type and extensiveness of the service, as well as with the area of the country and the prestige of the consultant. Outside the New York and Los Angeles markets, the fees for straight color analysis run between $35 and $45 per hour. Debra Lindquist's service includes a color analysis, from which she assembles a personalized packet of color swatches the client will use in selecting future wardrobes, and a styling seminar, all for a flat fee. "I charge $95 for a consultation here in the office. Sometimes, when I'm traveling out of town I charge more to cover extra expenses and commissions that I pay," she says.

Charges for personal shopping and closet evaluations range from $25 to $45 per hour. Debra often suggests that a client save money by doing some advance weeding and organizing so that she can look over the wardrobe quickly.

Fees for executive or media image consulting can run up to $150 to $200 an hour.

It always pays to check into what others are charging for comparable services. If your fees are too much higher, you'll be undercut; on the other hand, too-low fees not only diminish your profits but also tend to make clients doubt the quality of your service.

Advertising

"You constantly have to figure out how you're going to keep this flow of clients coming. It's not like I'm open now and everybody just comes filing in automatically. You always have to be promoting."

Debra Lindquist

Because image consulting is such an attractive business for entrepreneurs, and one that's relatively easy to get into, you may be faced with some fairly stiff competition. As Judy Ruckstuhl points out, "With a color consultant on practically every corner, the consumer is barraged with alternatives which can be pretty confusing." As a consultant, you must find some way of distinguishing yourself, some method of attracting the attention of your prospective clients. Happily, there are numerous effective promotional tools from which to choose.

- Many color consultants start with a simple phone directory listing. For a slightly higher charge, you can have your business name printed in bold type.

- You might work out a reciprocal referral arrangement with local clothing stores and beauty shops.

- Offering freebies such as gift certificates for weddings and graduations can bring lots of referral business; if the bride is pleased with her own look, she might urge her entire wedding party to go for their own consultations.

- Charity organizations often need raffle and door prizes for their fund-raising events. Offering your services brings favorable publicity and helps build an association in the minds of the public between you and the influential people in your community.

- You can volunteer your services as a speaker for conferences and seminars. If there is a support group in your area for women re-entering the job market, you could arrange to be a member of the consulting board.

- Debra Lindquist offers a free introductory class called "Confused with Color," which gives prospective clients a chance to compare her own Color Profiles with other color systems. You might also invite local fashion retailers to your introductory class and offer help in using the color packets their customers bring to their stores.

- You can do direct mailings to specific groups that would be likely to benefit from your service. Women's business networks are especially good sources of mailing list names.

- Cultivate repeat business. Be sure to keep a mailing list of previous customers whom you can invite to return for fashion or accessory updates once or twice a year.

- One of the best forms of advertising is a newspaper feature story, which can be fairly simple to set up, especially if you're doing a consultation for a prominent member of the community. The next best thing to such an article would be to furnish the paper with your own press release.

- Judy Ruckstuhl bylines a weekly fashion column for a newspaper in her area. The column offers tips to readers and helps Judy establish an image of authority.

- Publishing a newsletter — even a two-page quarterly — is another way of building a reputation of being in the know about current trends.

- Is there a local TV station that has a noonday talk show or community calendar? Rather than pay for expensive TV advertising, see if you can get on such a show. One approach is to offer to color analyze the host on the air.

In the long run, the best advertising is an enthusiastic referral from a satisfied customer. You'll be delighted, as Judy Ruckstuhl was in a recent introductory class, to hear two women say, "We're here because a girl in our office looks so much better after having her colors done — and you're the people who did it!"

Monetary and Psychic Rewards

Image consulting is an excellent field for the person with an unusual combination of business savvy, artistic flair and interpersonal skill. Interest in image-polishing has grown to un-precedented levels, making it possible for you to convert your talents and know-how to sizable profits. What's more, there are psychic as well as monetary rewards involved. It's an exhilarating challenge to help clients achieve a look that works aesthetically, that says what they want to say and that fits their personalities and lifestyles. In a sense, you work with your clients to create living, dynamic works of art, three-dimensional expressions of their best feelings about themselves. When it all clicks, it is enormously grati-fying for both you and your clients.

You might have had some exposure to consulting through a retail or direct sales job, in which case you already know you like working closely with people. Going the next step and establishing your own consulting business adds a number of exciting, satisfying dimensions:

- Independence. You can call your own shots, make your own decisions and take full advantage of the kinds of ideas that often fall through the cracks when you work for a big company.

- You can choose your own clientele. Perhaps you've always wanted to work with entertainers, or helping executives make the most of their personal assets might be your forte. In your business, you can specialize in the kind of con-sulting you most enjoy.

- You'll have the freedom to work your own hours, to devise a schedule that allows for young children or for your own schooling.

- For Debra Lindquist, variety is one of the big attractions. "It's a varied kind of career. It's continually interesting, never boring or humdrum. I meet people in this career that I would never have met in any other capacity."

Finally, there is the satisfaction of helping others realize their potential which is so rewarding to those with a true "people" orientation, especially when a jump in self-esteem is part of the change. "It's rewarding," says Debra, "when you see people making big strides in changing their appearance and achieve levels of success that perhaps they wouldn't have without some of these changes.

"We had a lady one time who was about 80, but she was still interested in her appearance. [Afterward,] she wrote us a letter saying, 'Dear Miracle Workers, I feel better about my clothing than I've ever felt and I am excited to let you know that even my zest for living has improved!'

"I think colors can give a feeling of confidence and self-worth," says Debra. "People think, 'Hey, I'm really special! I can make me look good!' "

It's great to be part of that process.

Chapter 9
Writing and Editorial Services

There is something paradoxical about the opportunities in writing today. On one hand, only a tiny percentage of the book and article manuscripts submitted for publication actually see print, and the percentage of freelance writers earning a living from their efforts is correspondingly low. On the other hand, demand for concise written communications has never been greater and will continue to grow as we move further into the information age.

At the root of this paradox is the issue of specialization. Although many people take pride in their writing abilities and seek ways to be financially rewarded for their skills, most make the mistake of attempting to be a generalist in an increasingly specialized world. One result is that general-interest publications are inundated with unsolicited manuscripts while opportunities in more specialized types of writing often go begging.

Opportunities and Rewards

There are genuinely good opportunities for specialized writing and editing today, and prospects for growth in this field are excellent. In all types of specialized writing — including technical writing, promotional writing and instructional writing — the one skill that will open almost unlimited opportunities for you is the ability to interpret specialized subject matter for technical and nontechnical readers alike.

The financial rewards can be substantial. An article in *Writer's Digest* by Robert Bly, who specializes in industrial writing, included the following: "I know one freelancer who recently earned $15,000 for writing a brochure for a major defense contractor. It took him only three months to complete, and he was handling several other projects at the same time. Another freelancer I know charges $320 a day for writing 'case histories' — success stories about a company's products and plants. Recently I wrote a ten-minute film script on a management information system and earned $1000 for a rainy Sunday's effort."

As the *Writer's Digest* article points out, it's not necessary to have an engineering degree to take advantage of writing opportunities in fields like industrial sales promotion. What *is* required is the ability to write simply and clearly and the patience and willingness to learn about your subject matter.

The Question of Media

If you associate the information age with high-tech communications media such as video and fiber-optic communications, you may question whether writing skills will, indeed, continue to be in demand. N. J. Del Calzo, a public relations consultant whose firm serves clients from real estate, financial and management consulting, and state government, has some strong opinions on this. He believes that all communications, regardless of the form it eventually takes, have their roots in the written word. The message can be delivered on film or videotape, in a news broadcast, in a magazine article or brochure, but in any case, he says, "You need to start with the power of the written word and move from there to determine what channel you wish to use to reach a particular audience. . . . You cannot expect a carpenter to build a house without a hammer and a saw; we build communication with the use of words." This need for communication exists whether the client is a scientific research firm in need of an editor for its newsletter, a psychology professor seeking a publisher for his textbook, or a job-hunting field geologist shopping for a resume writer. In virtually every endeavor there is a built-in demand for the services you, the skilled wordsmith, can deliver. Your task is to determine where and how you can best market your skills.

A Sampling of Opportunities

There are untold numbers of gifted professionals who possess considerable expertise in their own fields but lack the ability to express themselves well on paper. There are others who write well but need help getting their work into print, and there are all types of organizations — large and small, profit and nonprofit — that require either on-going or occasional writing and editing services.

Business Writing

"Any publishing house, even the smallest, needs an editor. In every city — maybe not in Ainsworth, Nebraska, but certainly in Omaha, Nebraska — you're going to find them. There is just a crying need for good freelance editors and proofreaders and people with word skills."

— Carol Rasmussen

Carol Rasmussen left an editing job with a New York magazine to free-lance. Together with a friend, she created Precision Editorial Services and offers copywriting, editing, research, layout and production services to publishing houses and other businesses. The business is operated out of Carol's home. "I have a study, and that comes off the income taxes. All you basically need is a typewriter, a bunch of pencils, a few reference books and a telephone — and several changes of clothes so when you go out for interviews you don't have to wear the same thing every time. But the important thing is your experience. That's what you're selling people.''

Carol feels her background in the sciences has been an asset in finding clients from the engineering and research fields. Businesses in these fields, as well as virtually all other fields, have an ongoing need for writing as a marketing tool. Large companies will, of course, have their own marketing departments, complete with staff writers. Still, that leaves thousands of smaller firms with smaller budgets but essentially the same kinds of needs, and even the largest firms may occasionally need help with an overflow situation. Companies are willing to pay for a variety of different types of writing, including the following:

- Brochures
- Technical reports and manuals
- Articles for trade publications
- Business letters
- Staff training manuals
- Policy manuals
- Community outreach writing
- Annual reports

Ad Copywriting

At fees ranging from $25 to $50 and more per hour, ad copywriting is one of the most lucrative of all markets for freelancers.

At thirty-three, Carla Carwile's award-winning work for the health care and other industries has made her a highly successful copywriter. Carla is enthusiastic about her type of work and as she talks she occasionally taps her fingertips on the table top for emphasis. ''There are people who are corporate people and people who are not, and at this point in my life, I am not. Also, I wanted to create a setting in which I could have children and continue working.''

Carla wrote copy for a small agency before leaving to try freelancing. Like Carol Rasmussen, she works from an office in her home. At first she wanted to write only health care and humanistic pieces, but later she realized the value of being able to cross over to other fields. Now her extensive portfolio includes work for real estate and investment groups as well as health care organizations. "I think to limit yourself to something like health care — or energy writing a few years ago — without the ability to cross over is to limit your potential income." Carla recommends developing an awareness of all the opportunities that exist for freelance writing. "One way of creating a broader vision for yourself is to start being aware of every printed piece you see. Look at everything that's printed out there — the envelope stuffers in your bank statement, the brochures in your doctor's office — because someone has written everything that's printed, and there's no reason why you can't write more of it."

There are two separate approaches you can take to becoming an ad copywriter. The first is to develop your own client list. If you take this route — and assuming you don't have artistic as well as writing talents — you'll need to collaborate with an artist who can help you with the graphics and layout of your ads. One way to find clients is to look for poorly executed ads and then convince the businesses running the ads that you can do a better job.

The second approach is to work for advertising agencies on a freelance, contract basis. You won't have to worry about lining up clients or finding an artist you can work with if you take this approach, but you *will* have to do a good job of convincing the agency that you can write copy that will result in sales for the agencies' clients. The main tool you will use for this purpose is a portfolio of your best work.

If you are just starting out you won't have a portfolio of previous ad assignments, however. So what do you do? One solution is to take a selection of ads from a number of newspapers and magazines and improve upon them. The idea is to respond to the same marketing problem that the original ad attempted to address — but to do it better in every respect. If you're creative enough to do a good job of this, the creative directors of the ad agencies you approach should be able to recognize your skill and talent.

Another possibility is to develop a complete package of promotional and sales materials for a fictitious business and to use this as your portfolio. Such a package would include a well thought-out slogan, a few ads, some TV and radio spots, and possibly a billboard or two. The idea, of course, is to demonstrate as clearly as possible your ability to motivate consumers to respond to your creative ideas and persuasive writing abilities.

Once you've got a portfolio you should write to a number of agencies asking for an appointment to show your work. Robert Bly used a similar approach when he first began working with agencies. His letter to fifty of the largest ad agencies in the country only cost him $60, and it included a business response card. A 12 percent response rate, including assignments worth a couple of thousand dollars and several good sales leads, made the mailing well worthwhile.

Again, the pay for good ad copy is excellent. "Bill-able" hours include interviewing and conference time, research and actual copywriting time, and travel time. If you are especially fast you may want to charge by the project instead of by the hour — otherwise you will be paying a penalty for your speed.

Carla Carwile feels that $35 an hour is a fair, competitive rate. How much can a freelancer expect to gross the first few years? While she declined to quote her actual yearly income, she did say that her earnings, the first year on her own, did not drop at all from her previous year's salary "in the mid-20's." It will depend on your location and how hard you push yourself, but both Carla and Carol Rasmussen agree that the right person, with the right approach to carefully selected clients, can do extremely well as a freelance ad copywriter.

Newsletter Opportunities

Not only are there good opportunities for publishing newsletters today (see chapter 7), there are also good opportunities for producing newsletters on a freelance basis for organizations that lack the staff, know-how or inclination to do the job in-house. In addition to providing a steady income, freelance newsletter work can result in leads for articles you can sell to magazines and newspapers.

Probably the best way to line up freelance newsletter jobs is to persuade an organization that doesn't have a newsletter that there are numerous benefits to be gained from publishing one. You could stress the improved communication and public relations, either internal or external, or improved employee morale, for example. Whatever benefits you choose to stress, you should spell out exactly how such a newsletter would be produced, what it would look like, what it would accomplish, and so on. If you do a good job of persuading the organization that such a newsletter would be feasible and beneficial, it probably won't be difficult to convince them to let you put the first few issues together on a trial basis. Assuming you are able to uphold your end of the bargain, such a "trail" freelance arrangement can stretch into a long-term, regular source of income for you.

Whom should you approach with such a proposition? Almost any organization of any size, whether for profit or nonprofit, can be a potential newsletter client. Your local reference librarian can probably provide a list of organizations in your area, and may know of new organizations just being formed. You can also get leads about start-up organizations from articles in your local newspaper.

Once a client agrees to your proposal, you can charge by the hour or by the job. The per-hour rate will vary depending on where you live but it should be about the same as that charged by public relations writers in your area. Your duties for any particular newsletter job may include any or all of the following, and you should bill your clients accordingly.

- Meeting with clients to discuss ideas
- Researching ideas
- Calling to set up interviews
- Conducting the interviews
- Taking photos if necessary
- Writing
- Getting approval of your articles
- Rewriting when necessary
- Preparation of copy for typesetting

- Being the liaison with the typesetter
- Proofreading
- Layout and Pasteup
- Working with the printer to overcome any production snags

If you quote a flat rate instead of an hourly fee you should be careful to take into consideration the amount of start-up time the job will require. This includes the time you will need to become thoroughly familiar with the organization and the contacts you will depend on for interviews and story ideas. You may want to stipulate that the rate you are charging for the first issue may be adjusted if you find the job takes much longer than anticipated. Realize, too, that you can expect each issue to be a little bit easier and faster to produce than the last as you develop a thorough understanding of your subject matter and form a dependable network of contacts within the organization.

What kind of articles will you be writing for newsletters? Although it will vary depending on the organization, typical copy includes:

- news coverage
- columns or letters from officials in the organization
- short profiles
- humor
- short articles on the history of the sponsoring organization
- calenders of upcoming events
- reports on issues of ongoing concern
- notices of policy changes

Marjorie Wood and James Larris have gone a step beyond freelancing in preparing newsletters. Their Pasadena, California-based company, "Newsletter Specialists," advertises in the *Los Angeles Business Journal,* the *Los Angeles Times*, and local accounting magazines for new clients. Marjorie, quoted in an *In Business* article, explained that "Newsletters are good for targeting an audience and are a very subtle promotional tool for companies that don't like to advertise, but are faced with increasing competition, like C.P.A.'s, doctors and lawyers.'' Newsletter Specialists offers three basic services:

- Full Service: To provide all interviewing, photography, writing, layout and pasteup, typesetting and printing, Newsletter Specialists charges a flat fee of $300 per page.

- Shared Service: If the client provides the written, technical copy and Newsletter Services does everything else, a fee of $200 per page is charged.

- Editing and Production: If copy and artwork are the client's responsibility, Newsletter Services will provide editing and production for a fee of $100 per page.

A one time start-up fee of up to $500 is charged new clients to cover design costs. After two years in business Newsletter Specialists had a dozen full-service clients.

Resumes

While a changing economy can be frustrating — and scary — the positive flip side is the creation of new jobs, with people moving from one occupation to another, getting more training, jockeying for the best opportunities. The more competitive the field, the greater the need for sophisticated marketing on the part of the job applicant. Job hunters' willingness to pay well for sharp, hard-selling resumes that display their credentials in the best possible light has made resume writing one of the more lucrative of the free-lance options.

One wordsmith who has tapped this market is David Francis Curran. Reporting on his experience in *Writer's Digest* magazine, David wrote ''Although business has its seasonal ups and downs I've made as much as $125 in a day. It's not far-fetched to expect resume writing to produce a steady, dependable part-time or full-time income for any writer who learns the trade.

''Learning the trade'' is not especially difficult. Success hinges on your ability to condense information about your client into succinct, interest-grabbing copy that will convince the prospective employer that your client is the one he should interview. Three basic steps are involved in explaining to the employer how your client might be of value to him:

- You must first understand the employer's business. What is he looking for in an employee?

- You must gather basic information about your client, usually through a questionnaire. A personal interview will provide you with the specific details you'll need.

- Finally, you must organize the information into a concise, visually impressive format — preferably no more than two pages. Remember that there is no "correct" format, so choose the one that reflects your client's qualifications in the best possible light.

How do you line up clients? The "Help Wanted" section of your local paper's classified ads — especially on Sundays — can be a highly effective source of business. A simple, inexpensive ad can persuade potential clients to give you a call and you can "sell them" on the benefits of your service over the phone. It's a good idea to take the client's name and phone number when setting up the appointment to ensure that he is serious and will show up.

Cover letters to accompany the resume can be an added sideline to your business. A good cover letter is addressed to a specific individual, explains what position is being applied for (and why), introduces the resume, and asks for an interview. With practice you'll find that you can produce such a letter in minutes.

Qualifications

Top-notch language skills are the premier qualification for success in freelance writing or editing. Like the pianist who practices scales each day to keep his technique solid, the writer's skill with words must be almost second nature. Communicating ideas is challenging enough without having to grapple with grammatical problems at every turn. Does that mean you need a degree in English? Not necessarily. The end product is the client's main concern, and if you know your craft and do a good job, that is the important thing. If your educational background hasn't adequately prepared you, there are other ways to sharpen your skills.

Excellent books on writing, such as *The Elements of Style*, by William Strunk, Jr., and E.B. White; *On Writing Well*, by William Zinsser, and Robert Morseberger's *Commonsense Grammar and Style* can all be tremendously helpful. Most colleges offer writing courses which can be taken either on campus or by correspondence. Writers' seminars and workshops can also be well worthwhile.

While all of the above are good places to start, many successful writers feel that the craft of writing is not something you can fully learn in school. "To learn to be an editor," says Carol Rasmussen, "you do it on the job. ... If you're working someplace where you know a good editor and you can see what they do and especially if they look at your work and tell you what they would have done differently — that's a great way to learn." Carla Carwile strongly agrees. "I feel I owe a great deal to a woman with whom I worked. I feel I had a natural talent to begin with, but having someone editing my copy, critiquing, fine tuning it, has been invaluable." "I did not learn to write in college," N. J. Del Calzo says. After I got my bachelor's degree, I worked for a metropolitan daily newspaper in St. Louis, and I spent five years with them learning to write." So don't be discouraged if you lack credentials. With study and practice, you can acquire the skills you need, and that's what's important.

Apart from technical ability, there are certain personality traits that can give you an edge over the competition. Carla Carwile feels that the most important trait a writer must have is the ability to listen, "to get in, to ask the right questions, to think about it — to really hear what is being said." That depth of listening and understanding requires that you have a sincere interest in people and a healthy curiosity about life in general. And it won't hurt if you like to study; you're likely to spend a great deal of time at the library, pouring over what's already been written on your subject. It's always a good idea to gather more data on your subject than you'll need so you can be selective.

It's true that writing ad copy for industrial heat pumps or editing a newsletter on changes in U.S. tax law may not be as glamorous as freelancing articles for large circulation general-interest magazines. It's also true that you are much more likely to be able to survive and prosper writing for more specialized markets — where the real opportunities are found today.

Chapter 10
Household Services

One of the side effects of the increasing numbers of women in the work force is a steady growth in the demand for housekeeping services. Although most people probably don't realize it, there are excellent opportunities for going into business in this field today.

Success stories are not hard to find. Consider the following examples:

- When Carol Brothers had trouble finding a maid, she started a cleaning service called Pop-Ins. During her first five years in business she sold thirty-two franchises at $22,500 each.

- David Labs quit a position as senior vice president of a large company in Milwaukee to start his "White Glove Maid Service." In just two years his gross income from this and his related business, "Royal Building Maintenance Co.," approached $250,000.

- Leone Ackerly was 31 when she launched her housecleaning business with an investment of $5. Before she turned 40 her company, Mini Maid Services, Inc., had scores of franchises and was a multimillion dollar business.

Mary Starkey's Experience

At 5:30 p.m. the office of Starkey and Associates is quiet, the staff having gone home for the evening. The office — four cinnamon-carpeted rooms filled with new furniture, shiny typewriters and Norman Rockwell prints — hints at the success Mary Starkey has found.

The murmur of voices can be heard down the hall; Mary is interviewing a young couple who have come in for help finding a housekeeper. With a new baby expected soon, they'll need an extra pair of hands around the house, but not just anyone will do. The husband wants a nonsmoker, the mom-to-be needs someone with energy and initiative, and both agree the person must love children.

Starkey and Associates began three years ago as a one-woman housecleaning service and is now one of the largest services of its kind in the state. Two basic services are offered: a residential cleaning service comprised of thirty subcontracted workers who clean 150 homes on a regular basis; and a domestic placement service through which Mary finds "household professionals" — maids, nannies, housemen, chefs — to work in private homes.

Mary's background doesn't fit the entrepreneurial stereotype. At nineteen she left college after one year to get married. When she and her husband divorced in 1975, she was left with little money, no job skills and two young children to support. "I was a South Dakota country bumpkin," she says. "I'd never had a job in my entire life, and I was scared to do anything." She heard about a work-study program at a local college that would provide her a small income while she earned a degree in social services. It sounded like just what she needed. She went through the program, received her degree and became a social worker in a shelter for retarded adults, gradually working her way up to a $19,000-a-year lobbying position. Many people would have been content with that accomplishment, but for Mary, the money and security weren't enough. She had expected to be of real service, to really help people, and in her view, the systems simply weren't helping enough. Discouraged and disillusioned, she left her job. It was back to square one, without a clue as to where to go next. For the time being, she felt, she needed time to think.

Again, she says, there was the problem of making ends meet. "A friend said to me, 'why don't you become a go-fer at our construction company until you figure out what you want to do?' So I did. I spackled a little and painted ceilings and did all kinds of stuff, and everybody thought I was totally crazy. But somewhere along the line I realized there was a need for cleaning at construction sites and that led to cleaning houses. I knew how to do that from watching the cleaning lady at home." In January 1981, Mary put an ad in the paper and got thirty calls the first week. Within six weeks she was making $300 a week as a cleaner. After two months, Mary got a call from a woman who had noticed her ads and wondered if Mary would help her find cleaning jobs. Mary agreed to find jobs for the woman in exchange for a percentage of her pay. "Wonderful!" the woman said. "You handle all the problems — I'll just clean the houses." Simply put, one thing led to another and, after sixteen months, Mary had eight workers and thirty clients.

Who Needs a Cleaning Service?

Who doesn't, from time to time, wish for a little help with the household chores? For as long as most of us can remember, having one's own cleaning lady has been regarded as the height of luxury and one of the earmarks of worldly success. Be that as it may, a factor that has played a significant part in the success of services like Mary Starkey's is the recent change in people's attitudes toward housecleaning services. Today's increasingly fast-paced lifestyle leaves people feeling caught up in the demands of work, home, family and social life, and more and more people are coming to view houshold help not as a luxury, but as an essential which deserves an important place in the family budget. As a result there is unprecedented demand for these services today.

Who are your potential customers?

- Single parents (both mothers and fathers)
- Two-career couples — especially those with young children
- Women, especially mothers, who attend school or serve in volunteer organizations
- New or expectant mothers
- The elderly or handicapped
- Those wanting an annual spring cleaning
- Owners of rental property

As you can see, some of your prospective clients will have more or less constant needs for your services; others will have only occasional or seasonal requirements. As a group, they make up a strong market for your services.

What Services Will You Offer?

Housecleaning services for residences — which can involve one person or a team visiting weekly or bi-weekly — usually provide a basic package, including vacuuming, dusting, floor cleaning, scrubbing bathrooms, washing kitchen cabinets and baseboards. For an additional charge you may want to add special projects, such as:

- cleaning ovens and refrigerators and washing windows.

- bigger jobs, such as cleaning fireplaces, rug shampooing, floor waxing, garage or patio cleaning, trash removal.

- services for commercial accounts and rental properties might also include painting and making minor repairs.

Housecleaning services usually don't get involved with daily dishes or picking up toys (usually the family or the family's nanny prefers to take care of these smaller tasks). Doing the family laundry is generally not practical for housecleaning services because so much time is spent waiting on washer and dryer cycles.

One important aspect of the services you offer is continuity, the assurance to your customer that, come what may, the work will get done. You eliminate the worry over whether someone will be there each week and whether the job will be done right. "I try to provide uninterrupted service," says Era Triggs, who, as head of Home Management Services, subcontracts cleaners to work in teams. "The homeowner doesn't have to be bothered with turnover. If someone quits, I replace him and train the new person myself."

Era feels another important feature of her cleaning business is the personalized service she gives each of her customers. "When I solicit a new client, I visit them; they tell me the things that are important to them; I tell them what we do. The first time the cleaners go to the home, I go through the home with them, point out all the things that need to be done, and sometimes actually work with them."

Placement Services

A logical growth step is into domestic placement, meaning that you find permanent or semi-permanent household workers — maids, housemen, nannies — for your clients and charge a finder's fee (generally the equivalent of one month's salary for the worker.) Mary's business now specializes in this service, which offers some distinct advantages to both her customers and the workers they ultimately hire.

Mary starts by interviewing the prospective employer, sorting out what he or she wants in the way of skills and personality. Often, she says, the client doesn't really know what is needed, so part of her job is helping write the job description. Mary says clients frequently expect too much for too little pay, in which case she counsels them on what can reasonably be expected.

Once she's determined what kind of help the customer wants, she obtains a deposit — about $250 — and then sets about finding just the right person for the job. She provides the advertising, screens the applicants, checks references, and finally sends the two or three best qualified, best suited people to the client, who interviews them and makes his own final selection. Once the worker is hired, Mary extends a two-month guarantee which states that if for some reason the arrangement doesn't work out, she'll find a replacement at no extra charge. She saves her customer a great deal of time and trouble, and, since she has an acute sense of what to look for in an applicant, she gives him the best chance of hiring the right person.

Mary feels that she also helps the household worker through her efforts at upgrading the nature of the job. In the past, housecleaning was a low-pay, low-self esteem kind of work. "I try to make the job as professional as I possibly can: taxes taken out, paid holidays, paid vacations — just like a regular job — so it's not a babysitting job, or a 'frump housecleaner' job, or a situation where you're a slave." She also makes an effort to ensure that employees are placed in compatible households. "I try to match people up with similar backgrounds. I won't put a smoker in a non-smoking household. I won't place a black worker in a house that has difficulty with minorities."

Should I Work Alone or Hire Helpers?

Caroline Gromosaik calls herself "The Domestic You'd Swear Was Imported." After deciding that secretarial work was not her cup of tea, she put together her own one-woman residential cleaning service. In addition to making a sizable income, Caroline enjoys some great fringe benefits:

- Freedom to work as many or as few hours a week as she wants.
- Flexibility in scheduling working hours, days off, and vacations.
- Independence: She relies only on herself; is solely responsible for the quality of her work.
- She chooses her own clients. She has become personal friends with a few and is frequently invited along on theater and symphony outings.

There are also advantages to the team approach to housecleaning. Comradery often works to make every team member want to carry his fair share of the load, and an experienced, well trained team can work with almost blinding speed. Such teams can, of course, handle a much larger number of houses. And if a team member gets sick, someone else can always fill in.

Start-up Costs

Lack of capital is not an overwhelming obstacle in starting a housecleaning service. Naturally you'll need a consistent source of income for living and business expenses while you get established, but since the service is almost completely labor intensive you won't need a lot of cash up front. Mary Starkey, you'll recall, got started with virtually no capital investment, using her own wages as a cash flow and letting the business pay for its own growth. Initially you'll need only a bare minimum of equipment and supplies.

- A telephone is the only office equipment which is absolutely essential. You may want to add a business line to your home phone.

- Your needs for promotional materials will largely depend on the market you're approaching. For Caroline, who works alone and specializes in private residences, a simple business card is sufficient. If you plan to compete for commercial cleaning contracts, on the other hand, a professionally prepared brochure describing your services would be an asset.

- Stationery and envelopes probably aren't necessary. Your billing statements can be left at the home when the job is finished.

- Transportation requirements will depend on the size of your operation. Caroline cuts her expenses to the bone by using public buslines; she schedules her appointments according to the geographic area. If you decide to use cleaning teams, it might be worthwhile to invest in a reliable second-hand van or station wagon (also useful if you plan to use your own cleaning equipment).

- Special cleaning equipment, such as ladders, rug shampooers, floor waxers, etc., can be rented at first and purchased when justified by the volume of your business.

- Most cleaners arrange for the client to provide cleaning supplies, and are careful to let the client know when supplies are running low. If you plan to take on special projects like window washing or carpet shampooing, however, you may want to provide your own supplies.

- You may or may not decide to set up an office. The main consideration is whether you go to your customers or they come to you. Caroline obviously needs no office. Although Era Triggs has a nice home office, she says she generally prefers to conduct business from her kitchen, using just her pocket-size Daytimer and the business line of her home phone. Mary worked from her bedroom for months, but moved to an office when she decided to expand her business to include a domestic placement service. Although she started with two modest rooms in a commercial building, her first office provided a place to interview clients and prospective workers in addition to storage space for the business records she needed to keep. Later, after her placement service really took off, she moved upstairs to more spacious quarters.

- Advertising can be very simple and inexpensive. Services specializing in private residences generally use newspaper ads, although once you become established you may find the demand so great that word-of-mouth referrals are sufficient.

For spring cleaning projects, commercial contracts,

and special jobs where the demand is more seasonal or sporadic, you may find that a Yellow Pages ad will pay off. You can also send special mailers to prospective clients. Christmas cards to former customers can serve as a reminder that will bring repeat business.

Expansion

One of the trickier aspects of any business, expansion requires careful planning and a keen awareness of trends in your market. Vacations, the beginning and ending of the school year, and holidays are all factors which can have an impact on demand and are therefore important to consider when you're thinking about adding staff, equipment, or vehicles. "One of the problems people run into," says Mary Starkey, "is not having enough money to keep up with expansion. It's better to let the business create its own foundation than to force it." Mary points out that she added staff the same way she changed from her home to a small office and then to larger offices — she made the changes very gradually, only as needed, and based on the cashflow generated by the business.

What to Charge

Your charges will be determined by several factors: the services performed, whether you work alone or use a cleaning team approach, and the going rates in your area. The hourly rates for a single cleaner range between $7.50 and $15 per hour, with a three-hour minimum. Caroline found herself so much in demand that she decided to limit her clientele by raising her rates above what she guessed people would be willing to pay. To her surprise, many people in her area were perfectly willing to pay $9 per hour. Interestingly enough, Caroline notes, the customers most able to pay top wages are frequently those whose homes need the least upkeep.

It is customary to charge a flat rate for cleaning teams; the cost is based on what the customer wants done each time, how long the job will take, and how many people work on the team. Fees usually vary between $22.50 and $55 per visit, although they can go substantially higher for unusually large jobs like spring cleaning or cleaning up a rental property that tenants have vacated.

You'll need to learn how to estimate the cost of a project so that you stay competitive without cutting margins too close to make a profit. Era Triggs feels that skillful bidding is simply part of a good service. "I feel that it's real important to be honest with people, and if you can't do the job for a price they can afford, you'd best tell them that. . . . It's important that the job comes in very close to what I estimated — and if I make a mistake, I eat it."

Tips for Success

Mary Starkey stresses the importance of a service-oriented attitude toward the business. "On all levels, if you try to deliver the best service rather than wring dollars, people naturally come across." Next on the list, she feels, would be a professional approach:

- Dress for success. If possible, wear a business suit when estimating jobs. Caroline arrives at her client's home in fashionable streetwear, then changes into her work clothes for the job itself.

- Get a good, comprehensive work order that is clear to both parties. Make sure your workers understand exactly what is expected of them.

- Follow up. Many cleaners provide a checklist for the customer to fill out in order to make sure each task was done satisfactorily — and if something wasn't done right, the workers are sent back.

- Your own hands-on experience is important. Mary believes her own experience as a cleaner has given her indispensable insight. "I know what turned me on about a cleaning client and what made me angry; what made me do a good job or a bad job. I can communicate this to my clients, help them have a better working relationship with their cleaners."

What to Look for in Your Workers

As previously mentioned, working alone gives a person complete control over the quality of the service; taking on helpers means you'll relinquish some of that control. To maximize the likelihood of customer satisfaction with your service it is critical that you choose your workers carefully. In addition to the basic skills required, there are some special qualitites to look for in the people who will represent your service to your clients. The ideal worker is trustworthy and reliable, with a clean, neat appearance and a positive, pleasant attitude. Because your workers will be going into private homes you have a responsibility to thoroughly check their references and previous work history.

Avoiding Pitfalls

As in any labor-intensive business, your biggest challenge will be keeping your workers as well as your customers happy. This calls for good public relations skills and an awareness of the problems you might encounter.

- High turnover. No matter how good the circumstances, it's a rare individual who will be content in the job indefinitely; for most people, housecleaning will be an interim job. Still, there are things you can do to win your workers' loyalty and decrease turnover. Mary believes the thing workers value most is fairness. "I knew they were doing most of the work so I felt they should receive most of the money. So I paid my workers 75 percent and kept 25 percent. Because of that, I have the best cleaners in town."

  Occasional misunderstandings or personality clashes are fairly inevitable; communication — the three-sided variety among yourself, your customers and your workers

— is essential. It is a serious mistake to automatically assume that your client is right and your worker is wrong.

- Illness. You'll need some kind of provision for getting the work done when your workers call in sick. It will happen sooner or later, so you should plan for it from the beginning.

- Transportation breakdowns. A regular maintenance program will minimize the likelihood of breakdowns, but you'll probably have a few to deal with in spite of your precautions. Be prepared when it happens.

- Theft. Unfortunately, theft is a fact of life. Some services ask their workers to sign a document agreeing to take a polygraph test if it should become necessary.

- Business ups and downs. "All businesses have cycles," says Mary. "Just because it's big in December doesn't necessarily mean it will be big in January. Each city and part of the country has its own cycle." By anticipating slumps and peak periods, you can adjust your activities so you won't get caught with high expenditures in a period of low cashflow.

"Good Money" — and More!

Asked why she left a high-paying job as executive chef with a first-class restaurant chain to strike out on her own, Era Triggs replied, "I wanted to have the ceiling lifted off my income. When you work for someone else, they always determine what you make and what your job description will be. I wanted the flexibility to do some of the things I want to do while serving the needs of other people." Has the business met her expectations? "The money is good — it took only two months to put it together and get it rolling, and it began showing a profit after only four months — and it's allowed me to spend more time with my family. But I think I get the most satisfaction from seeing people pleased with the service they've received."

"It's teaching me so much," says Mary Starkey. "By watching the business, I'm learning about people, about life, about myself. My children are getting the benefit of my being more balanced."

Owning your own housecleaning service could mean a chance at the kind of income, the kind of lifestyle and the personal satisfaction you want from your work. The opportunities are there now, and all indications are that the market will only grow stronger as more and more women — the traditional housecleaners — enter the workforce.

Chapter 11
Educational Services

The last decade has brought major changes in business and industry, where not just new jobs, but whole new fields have been created as a result of shifting cultural trends. One such trend, the growing tendency of people to look less to institutions and more to themselves for necessities like employment, medical care, and education, has led to the formation of thousands of new businesses. This chapter will explore some of the services that have sprung up in response to rising demand for alternative sources of education.

College Enrollments Down; Seminars, Minicourses Up

While it's true that college enrollments have suffered during the last ten years, people want education now more than ever. What has changed most is that people no longer put blind trust in traditional sources to provide the education they want. Traditionally, we've looked to institutions to tell us what we need to know and how we should go about acquiring that knowledge. Many of us got a big shock, however, when we entered the job market only to find that our schooling inadequately or inappropriately prepared us for the real world. Now more and more people, and especially adults in their thirties and forties, are saying, "Look, I have my own ideas about the kind of knowledge and training I need, and I can make my own decisions about who can best provide it." As a result, substantial profits are being made by those who can supply the right kinds of education in formats that are fast, cheap, and readily accessible. *Venture* magazine reports that in one recent two-year period, "Educational services generated the highest number of [small business] startups . . . . For companies with fewer than 100 employees, that segment grew 26 percent annually, creating 9,086 new establishments during that time."

In addition to growing consumer demand, there is another reason for the success of private educational services: their appeal to teachers who have become disillusioned with their role within institutions and with bureaucracies that tend to place obstacles in the way of learning. Now, gifted individuals with access to useful information can sidestep the rules and red tape imposed by school administrators and simply teach. They can often make a better living on their own than by slugging it out with taxpayers in a society that has long paid lip service to the value of education while keeping teachers among the lowest-paid professionals. It's not uncommon for a freelance teacher, as an entrepreneur, to make $100 to $300 per hour, or for an independent seminar consultant to make $900 in a day. Sound appealing? Then let's take a look at some of the opportunities.

Seminars

One of the fastest-growing new educational services is the seminar business. "Because the industry is so fractionated, no one is sure just how large it is," reported Eli Spielman in *Venture*. "But a confidential market study by General Motors Corp. estimates that approximately 40,000 seminars are given annually in the United States and Canada, with estimated revenues of between $100 million and $160 million." Seminar customers are a breed very similar to newsletter subscribers: people willing to shell out big fees — $200 to $500 — for a two-day dose of concentrated, practical, preferably inside information that can be directly applied to their businesses.

"One of the major concerns of any corporation right now is the productivity of the individual employee," says Hyrum W. Smith, whose firm produces the corporate seminar, "Focus on Time Management." "If they can send somebody to a class that will guarantee an increase in productivity, they can't afford not to do it." So far, over thirty companies, including Merrill Lynch, Dow Chemical, and Nike, have decided that indeed they can't afford to pass up Smith's seminar. What kind of person benefits most? Basically, anyone with the responsibility of establishing his or her own work structure: salesmen, executives, entrepreneurs. But the class doesn't appeal only to business people; it's also been given to nursing groups, and there is currently a growing demand for the seminar among homemakers. Many of the people who attend the corporate seminars, according to Smith, convince their spouses to attend the public seminars. "Time management is one of the most universal topics there is; it touches everybody."

What it Takes

If you've ever attended a motivational seminar, you know that it can be an exhilarating experience for both teacher and classmember. Often the ideas presented aren't anything new, but the manner in which they're presented — with interesting anecdotes, jokes, problem-solving exercises, learning games — is extremely appealing. It's fun, and it tends to look easy. But, warns Smith, don't be fooled by the talented seminar trainer who makes it look like a cinch. "A lot of guys get excited about doing this, then go out and teach their first corporate seminar and get creamed." The reason, he believes, is that it's not enough just to have good concepts; the trainer must be able to relate the information in ways that can be quickly grasped, that make strong, lasting impressions, and, most importantly, that motivate the participants to action.

Smith points out that unlike teaching in an academic setting, where the emphasis is 90 percent content and 10 percent delivery, teaching corporate seminars requires 50 percent content and 50 percent delivery. "You see, the professor at the university never has to worry about his students [not] coming back. They have to. In a corporation, they *don't* have to come back, so when you go into a corporation and charge them $5,000 for a two-day seminar, you'd better really be good." Smith feels it's important that the participant enjoy the learning process, that he be "a little bit entertained while he's learning." That takes a special combination of sharp intellect — the ability to remember faces, to articulate ideas well, to think on your feet, field questions — plus a magnetic, persuasive personality. If you've got these traits, and if you're willing to commit yourself to a period of building your business, the seminar field could be a good choice for you.

Preparing Yourself

A college degree is not necessary. "I don't think I would say that X or Y educational background was best," says Smith, whose Focus consultants come from varied backgrounds in sales, education, and business management. "The most important issue is platform skills, the ability to read how you're being perceived by your audience. I can teach somebody what they need to know to teach the class; it's a whole lot tougher to teach them platform skills."

"I think it takes a big ego," Smith continues. "Like tomorrow, I'm talking to 400 executives who're each paying 500 bucks for a two-day seminar. When people pay that kind of money, you have to be pretty confident in your ability to turn them on. You've got to have a very outgoing personality — confident, but not cocky."

You must truly believe in the concepts you teach, too, and people must be able to see the results of implementing what you teach in your own life. "If you're not following the program yourself," says Smith, "your credibility goes right down the drain."

Teaching or sales experience can be especially helpful both in acquiring public speaking skills and polish and in developing contacts. In fact, the best training may be working for a time as a consultant for an established seminar firm where you can learn the ropes.

Testmarketing Your Idea

> *"Bad marketers begin with a product or a service and ask the question, 'How can I sell it?' Good marketers start with the market and say, 'What does the market want?' and then design the product or the service to fit the demand of the marketplace."*
>
> —Howard L. Shenson

The same testmarketing principles that apply to hand lotions and chocolate chip cookies also apply to seminars, according to Howard L. Shenson, a consultant and publisher who teaches a seminar on the seminar business. "What you have in the seminar field is a group of people I would call hapless inventors, who spend years, sometimes, developing seminar programs only to discover that they don't sell." Which is unfortunate, because it's a fairly simple and inexpensive matter to test a concept before spending huge amounts of on materials and promotion. Shenson offers the following tips:

- Test your seminar in a small market.

     "Many people think they want to test a seminar in a very large market, Los Angeles or New York or Denver. But the costs of advertising and conducting seminars are much higher in such markets than they are in others. So the solution for testing seminars is not to come to Los Angeles and spend five to ten thousand dollars. The solution is to go to a much smaller market — Albuquerque, Santa Barbara, northern New Jersey . . ."

- Start with a modest promotional campaign, then build.

     "You can test any seminar concept for a thousand dollars or less," asserts Shenson. "Since promotional costs represent 70 percent of the total cost of conducting a seminar, let's set aside $700 for, say, a test mailing. If it costs $.30 to $.35 per person you reach, you're going to reach 2,000 to 2,100 people for your seven hundred dollars."

Shenson goes on to explain that if you get a response to the mailing which brings in revenues equal to three times the cost of your mailing, that would be a fair indication that your seminar will sell (in this case, that would mean twenty registrants at $105, or ten at $210, for a total of $2,100). "If you can return $2,100 on your investment of $700, the next time you can go out and spend $7,000 if you want and probably return $21,000. But most people make the mistake of going out and saying, 'Well, let's see, I want to have fifty people at this seminar, therefore I'm going to mail 20,000 pieces of mail,' and they find that their seminar is not marketable or that their marketing approach is wrong and now they've spent eight, ten, twelve thousand dollars finding that out."

No matter how well your idea sells, however, you should count on updating and refining your curriculum on a regular basis. One of the most effective and cost-sparing methods of fine-tuning your program is to use evaluations by classmembers. "In every seminar we teach," explains Hyrum Smith, "we have every person in the seminar write a written critique, so we now have thousands of critiques. We have, quite frankly, done considerable refining as a result of the comments people have made."

In any case, it's always wise to experiment several times with a new idea before spending the money to make it part of the program by way of additions to a student guide book or expensive computer graphics slides.

What to Charge

Registration fees vary widely — between $45 for a half-day public seminar and $500-plus for a two- or three-day corporate program. What you charge will depend on your expenses, the value of the seminar information to your registrants, and the prevailing rates in your area. Your expenses will likely fall into three categories:

- Operating costs: air fare, lodging, conference room rental, meals — both your own and a banquet lunch for your registrants.

- Materials: student manuals, overhead projector slides and other visual aids, copies of books and handouts, shipping of materials to conference locations.

- Promotional costs: design, printing and postage of brochures or direct mail fliers; charges for mailing lists, long-distance phone calls.

Expanding Your Operation

If you've come up with a winning idea for a seminar, and you've promoted it effectively, chances are you'll soon find yourself with more requests for seminars than you have time to teach yourself. At some point you'll want to take on additional trainers or consultants to help handle the load and the best approach is to subcontract with these individuals. Hyrum Smith, who subcontracts with eight independent consultants, believes there are several advantages to this arrangement.

For one thing, subcontracting keeps overhead at a minimum. "We save $50,000 a year by not having to pay their FICA taxes," explains Smith. "And it's an advantage to them. They have mastery over their own financial destiny; they can work their tax situations out the way they want to."

Since the consultants also act as a sales force, generating their own clients, they increase the overall volume of business. You profit not only from your own seminars, but also from each seminar taught by your staff.

Another advantage to subcontracting instead of employing your staff is that it allows you access to capable people who can teach only on a part-time basis. College professors, sales people, and other professionals, for example, might have only half a dozen discretionary days each month. All can make strong additions to your organization, and you pay them only when they teach for you.

Accessory Sales

Sales of accessory materials, such as cassette tapes, books, and correspondence courses, can really boost your income. In fact, says Howard L. Shenson, the more ways you can find to repackage your idea, the better. To increase profits from his "Focus on Time Management" seminars, Hyrum Smith markets cassette tapes of the seminar and a customized daily schedule and appointment book, called the Franklin Dayplanner. Sales of these items help smooth out the peaks and valleys of income from seminars. "The Dayplanner is a significant piece of our income. . . . If somebody buys one, they'll buy one year every year after that. That's the annuity that grows for you."

Promoting Your Seminars

"Word-of-mouth is unquestionably the most powerful marketing tool you have," claims Smith. "If your reputation has proceeded you into the company, selling them is relatively easy. We now have a pretty exciting list of clients, which gives us a very powerful third-party reference. If I'm talking to Dow Chemical and they say, 'Well, geez, who else have you taught?' — and they *always* want to know where else you've taught — I can tell them that we teach at Merrill Lynch, at Price Waterhouse, at Nike, and they say, 'Whoa — if you're teaching those people I'd better have you guys in.' "

But what do you do until you've built up that third-party reference list? The usual way to promote a public seminar is with newspaper ads. However, to sell a corporate seminar, it's better to zero in on the specific companies you want to attract with a combination of direct mail and personal contacts. Don't expect fliers alone to do it, says Smith. While a flier can get you in the door, it usually won't get you the contract. That takes a face-to-face closing session with a decision-maker, and *that* means lots of personal contacts. "The first year I was in the business I made a commitment to make twelve telephone calls every day that I wasn't teaching. It's a numbers game. After a while you start getting in to see people and you get your first corporate seminar, then your second . . . and now, in the last three years, I've probably taught in thirty corporations."

One helpful resource for newcomers to the seminar field is NASCAP, the National Association of Seminar Conference Providers and Arrangers, a nonprofit service organization which provides marketing and management assistance.

Minicourses

Currently, the biggest demand in the educational services field is for learning that is fast, inexpensive, and readily applicable. People want to go to the class this weekend and use their new knowledge on the job Monday morning. This being the case, it's not surprising that while college enrollments are down, the minicourse industry is booming. In fact, the market for minicourses is so broad-based and has grown so quickly that "learning networks" — companies that attract freelance teachers and offer their courses under one umbrella organization — have sprung up in many parts of the country. New York's "Network for Learning," for example, grossed $1.9 million and attracted 52,000 students in a recent twelve-month period, according to the *Wall Street Journal*."

One reason for the astounding popularity of minicourses is that promoters, who tend to look at students as consumers, constantly modify their class offerings and schedules in response to new demands. Although you can find an eight-hour course in virtually anything from hang gliding to wine tasting, the greatest demand seems to be for minicourses in subjects related to computers and health care (especially exercise and nutrition). One of the most popular courses at the Network for Learning is "Pregnancy After 30," a class which typically draws at least 250 people.

Successful as networks are, however, the field is still wide open to independents. Lucille Niebur, owner and founder of "Emergency Skills, Inc.," contracts with companies to teach employees how to handle medical emergencies like choking, seizures, bleeding, and shock in a series of eight three-hour sessions. The program, called "Alive," costs $200 per employee and so far has been taught in over sixty companies.

Computer Courses

The burgeoning computer field has generated an especially ripe market for minicourse teachers and promoters. Computers have become so commonplace in homes as well as businesses — and the growth has been so rapid — that neither salespeople nor consumers can keep up with the new technology being offered. New software is being introduced faster than people can learn to use it. There's a tremendous need for people with computer expertise who are also competent teachers.

"Our purpose is to provide a kind of warm and welcoming, safe space for people to be introduced to the world of microcomputers," says Ron Anastasia of The Computer Tutors. "We basically have two markets," he continues. "We have the novice user who's just getting introduced to microcomputers. Then we have quite a few professionals who want to upgrade their skills — some of them are mainframe professionals who want to get involved in microcomputers, or they already know microcomputers but they don't have the time to learn a new software package. Companies, especially, are realizing that their valuable professional employee's time is much better spent taking a good training course to learn a new software package . . . rather than playing around with it for two or three weeks on their own, using valuable company time."

In response to this dual market, Ron and his staff offer a selection of four-week minicourses: introduction to personal computers, basic programming, data base management, and word processing. There are also classes in new software, such as Lotus 1-2-3, along with a trio of minicourses for Apple Macintosh business applications. The student can choose the course that best suits his or her particular needs.

Each minicourse — mostly hands-on training — is comprised of four weekly, two-hour evening classes, and costs $80. Classes are limited to twelve students, with a maximum of three students per computer. Ron also offers customized training for corporations and personalized one-on-one tutoring "for subjects in which there isn't enough demand to create a whole public course." While personalized tutoring is much more expensive ($40 per hour compared with $10 per hour for classes), it's also much more concentrated. "We've discovered we can cover the same material in about half the time, because the tutor can focus on the individual student's speed and interests, and he's studying only the stuff that's of particular interest to him."

Cutting Costs: The Key to Profit

"We keep as many of our costs as we can variable and low, rather than fixed and high," says Ron. When he and Susan, his wife, first started their business three years ago, it was a big, impressive — and expensive — operation. Their store was in a 4,000-square foot mall location, with a full-time staff of ten and $50,000 worth of computer equipment. "It was a big operation," Ron fondly remembers. "We had all kinds of things going on — classes, private tutoring, a software library, a computer camp for kids — it was really great. But it cost us between $15,000 and $20,000 a month just in overhead, and the [local] computer training and rental market was just not large enough to support that kind of overhead."

"We learned a lot about business in those two years. We now operate with a much lower overhead. We operate out of an office in our home; we rent classroom space on just the evenings that we need it rather than having to pay twenty-four hours rent on a place. And we rent computers from our friends and bring over our own computer, so we only need to pay for the computers when we're using them, rather than day and night."

Streamlining his business, says Ron, has brought very positive bottomline results. "We're actually getting up to about the same number of people per month that we used to train with a storefront and with all that huge overhead. We're making money now where we were consistently losing money back then."

Another way Ron has quite effectively cut costs is by bringing in freelance computer teachers on a contract basis, rather than paying salaries (and benefits) to a full-time staff. Tapping local computer clubs, he adds, has been a great way of finding teachers. In fact, Ron hired instructors for his Apple Macintosh courses from the editorial staff of Club Mac. "Our staff is a really good group of people. We've trained on the order of 2,000 clients now, and we used to hand out student feedback sheets to our clients who would rank the teachers in a number of different dimensions on a scale of one to five. We would keep only the teachers who consistently got fours and fives. So they've proved themselves."

Advertising

Suppose you've researched the market and developed a curriculum that effectively meets existing demand. How do you get the word out? The important thing in allocating your advertising dollars is to pinpoint the groups which would be most likely to need your class. Here are some ways of reaching your potential students:

- Newspaper ads. In addition to daily newspapers, you might also consider the "alternative" news weeklies in your area. While circulations are smaller, advertising rates are correspondingly lower, and such papers generally appeal to a narrower demographic group. Choose a paper with a target market of primarily young urban professionals, for instance, and your advertising could be very cost effective.

- Special interest newsletters and magazines are another possibility. Many have listings of educational services.

- Brochures and mailers. One way of reaching your clients is to mail fliers to company personnel directors. They often know who in the organization could benefit from your type of class and probably will pass your flier along. You can also put posters on the bulletin boards of student centers, in employee lounges or in computer stores.

- Referrals. Don't hesitate to ask your minicourse participants for the names of friends who might also be interested. "We're getting more and more consulting referrals from our clients," says Ron. "It turns out that a significant number of the people who come to our classes are having problems bringing microcomputers into their professional environments and really need some consulting help. After they've taken a course and seen the competency of our teachers, they'll frequently ask if we can get involved with them on a consulting basis, and we do.''

Classes for Kids

As a young mother, Joan Barnes looked around her Bay Area community for organized activities that would be both stimulating and fun for her toddler, and she found that there really wasn't much available. So Barnes decided to develop her own program, something that would promote learning and make the most of youngsters' potentials at each stage of their development. The resulting program, Gymboree, has grown from a home-based part-time business to a million-dollar-per-year franchise, with nearly 200 centers nationwide.

What is Gymboree? Simply put, it is a weekly, 45-minute workout session for babies and toddlers aged three months to four years. The workout consists of a staff-led series of songs, games and maneuvers devised to promote sensory-motor development, balance, and coordination and to teach spacial concepts like "up," "under," and "through." In addition, youngsters benefit from social contacts with others — and especially from interaction with their parents. At Gymboree, parents aren't just onlookers but are active participants.

The fee for each twelve-week course is $48, or $4 per class. On any given day, some 10,000 youngsters and their parents come to the centers, which are usually housed in churches and community centers. Barnes, a former dancer, stresses that the idea behind Gymboree is not to produce little Mozarts or Einsteins, but rather to lay a foundation of skills that will facilitate future learning. As demonstrated by the remarkable success of the program, parents agree.

The fact is, Joan Barnes is just one example of the thousands of people who have created great careers out of educating the nations' young in nontraditional, noninstitutional settings. There are several reasons for the growth of this market. One factor is the increase in the number of working mothers and single parents, many of whom want to fill their children's after-school hours with something other than TV. Demand is also created by parents pursuing their own hobbies or education. Many feel that enrolling kids in fun, interesting activities during those hours makes sense, especially when considering that many of the programs cost no more than a baby-sitter. Then too, parents of the '80s tend to be older, more mature, more affluent; they can afford to enrich their children's lives with music lessons, computer camps, and special athletic activities. For many, having a family was a carefully planned choice — a choice that tends to rearrange priorities. Parents often make the decision to sacrifice "personal" time and material luxuries in order to invest in healthier, more secure, better educated children. For all these reasons, there is currently a tremendous need — which translates into business opportunities — for creative, child-oriented educators. Here are just a few of the people capitalizing on this growing trend:

- After School Workshops
    Sheila Bandman combines after school child care with cultural arts. In a cheerful, homey setting, kids can choose from a variety of activities such as reading, storytelling, arts and crafts, dramatics, puppetry, cooking, and carpentry. The atmosphere is relaxed and unpressured, and children are encouraged to do whatever interests them, even if that means only unwinding after school. The cost is $10 for a three-hour session.

- Language for Kids
    Nancy Conforti, a former teacher, makes learning a second language exciting for her young students. The program, developed by a team of language experts and early-childhood educators, makes teaching aids of games, puppets, posters, and toys. With only seven students to a class,

kids receive lots of personal attention. The cost: $85 for each nine-week session.

- Earthkeepers

    As an alternative to sports and summer school, Janet Sheldon offers a three-week creative arts workshop for children. In a summer day-camp format, kids learn about man's effect on the ecological balance of land, air, and water and begin to develop an awareness of how they themselves can care for the environment. Sheldon uses a variety of teaching methods — arts and crafts, storytelling, music, science projects — to introduce children to subjects like solar energy, gardening, and nutrition. There is also an overnight campout during the three-week, Monday-through-Friday program. The cost is $225.

Start-up Information

One of the best ways to promote a new course for kids is to offer the first class free. School counselors, teachers, and day-care moms can be helpful in getting the word out, and you may find that the only promotion budget you need is a few dollars you can spend on having a flier printed.

Because of the similarities between child-care services and children's classes, much of the start-up information provided in chapter four is applicable to this subject.

Avoiding Pitfalls

As in so many other services, the critical factors in education have to do with effective marketing and with keeping costs low. For all education services, the biggest pitfalls are in not researching the market adequately to make sure your idea will sell and in letting your overhead grow too big.

For seminar providers, the temptation will be to spend too much money developing the curriculum and on fancy promotional materials to use in selling it. It's important to start on a modest scale, testing the idea first in small markets and building on your success. Minicourse or special school operators need to avoid the trap of thinking that a fancy, expensive facility is necessary to attract students.

For all, there will be the continuing challenge of maintaining enthusiasm and avoiding burnout, especially if extensive travel is required. On the positive side, you'll have control of your own schedule. Hyrum Smith is careful to balance work with family life. "For one thing, I pick and choose when I travel. Like last week I took two days off and took my family to the mountains. I have the option to do that whereas most employees don't."

But for Smith, as for so many others, the real thrill is in the actual teaching experience. "What I'm really doing," he says, "is selling these people on making some changes in their lives. If I can get them to do that as a result of their sitting in my class, that's a real victory for me."

Chapter 12
Lawn and Garden Services

"Last week we had one of our dealers hit a million dollars. We've had two of them hit the half million mark. There is some money involved . . . ."
— Carl Lang, Director of Retail Marketing
Lawn Doctor

A number of trends are at work today that make self-employment in lawn and garden services an appealing and viable opportunity. Bob Early, publisher of *Lawn Care Industry*, points out that industry revenues have topped $2.2 billion and are growing at a rate of about 20 percent each year. In prime areas of the country, yard service professionals have more work than they can handle, and "it doesn't, frankly, take a lot of money for start-up," says Early. "If you have — or are willing to get — the knowledge, if you're willing to work hard, you can carve out a pretty good business for yourself."

A "Growth-Oriented" Business

One of the trends contributing to the opportunities in lawn and garden services is the growing recognition that money spent on landscaping and yard maintenance is actually an investment. As realtors often point out, investing in long-term improvements to your home can really pay off when you sell. To a certain extent, the growth of these services is self-perpetuating, too. "What the Jones have, the Smiths want," says the owner of Denver's Lawn Green service. "Our phones are ringing constantly."

The growing number of two-income households is another trend contributing to the growth of this field. With more discretionary dollars but less leisure time, people are buying more services in general; yard care, with its gratifyingly visible results, is one of the most popular. As Lawn Doctor's Carl Lang puts it, "When you have married people both working there's a pretty good income there. They're not going to be the do-it-yourselfers, the home gardeners." Our country's increasing retired population is another influencing factor. "Most older people don't want to putz around in the yard. With incomes a lot higher than they used to be, now maybe they want to go out and play golf or travel."

One major incentive for yard-care customers is the fact that it generally costs little if any more to hire a professional service than to do it yourself — "especially when you add in all of your time, the cost of the supplies and machinery, and the potential for misapplication by the homeowner," says Bob Early. "A hundred and fifty dollars a year is not a big expenditure to have your lawn looking nice."

Recession-Resistant

The lawn and garden industry has shown itself to be largely recession proof. ChemLawn Corporation, for example, has reportedly experienced as much as 25 to 30 percent growth during the last two recessions. Bob Early thinks he knows why. The typical yard-care consumer, who makes $25,000 a year or more and lives in the suburbs, is not significantly affected by recessions. Furthermore,

"When times are tight, people like to entertain more at home rather than take trips, so they spend more money making the place look nice inside and out. People get new drapes, put on a new coat of paint rather than go to the Rockies for a vacation. The attitude is 'let's spend the money on our own little place, our own little castle.' "

Tight money has been an even bigger impetus for the nonresidential customer. "In business, when you're scrapping for the tight dollars, you want to have your grounds looking nice so that people will buy your condos or rent your apartment, so people will come into your bank or restaurant."

Unrealized Potential

"One thing to remember," says Carl Lang, "is that the lawn care industry is just in its embryonic stage; a lot of people are beginning to think about using a lawn-care service, but 90 percent of the market is still untapped. There are still a lot of wide-open spaces yet to be cultivated." This isn't to say that everyone can expect to gross a million, Lang hastens to point out. A lot depends on the region of the country, the types of yards and gardens, and the degree of time and commitment the dealer wants to give. "A guy's got to go out there and hustle, but the point is, some of the people do it."

Of course, many people are not really looking for a Fortune 500 kind of venture anyway. You might want something you can do part-time, just to supplement the family income, build up your savings account, or put a child through school. In that case, says Lang, a yard-care business is a highly workable option. "One of our dealers is a retired military guy. He doesn't want anything big; he just wants to keep himself going in one particular section of his city, and that's all he wants to do. It's really up to the individual and how much he wants to put into it."

Fringe Benefits

Besides money, yard care provides a number of perogatives

that go with being your own boss — including the freedom to design your own operation and use your own ideas. As a yard-care professional, you can determine your own work schedule and be involved in all phases of the business from advertising and sales to actually providing your service.

In addition, opportunities in yard care offer a work environment that many people find appealing. Yard care offers the chance to get healthful exercise while working outside in the fresh air, and it is also a very versatile, flexible type of business that can be tailored to suit your own needs and ambitions. While some areas of the country — such as Florida — require year-round service, generally the business is somewhat seasonal. Some lawn-care service owners take advantage of the two- to three-month winter respite to gear up for spring. The slack time is used to update mailing lists or to have major work done on equipment. Others simply shift the emphasis from working on lawns and gardens to, say, snow removal. Still others enjoy the opportunity to work on home projects, to go skiing, or just relax.

Specialized Services

Kert Sorber has made a profitable business of one aspect of yard care — tree trimming. As in lawn chemical application, the demand for tree trimming is double based: Customers lack not only the time, but also the know-how to properly trim trees which often represent a major investment to property owners. "There's a lot more to it than just cutting off dead branches," says Kert. "You have to know where to trim to strengthen the tree." Having a landscape architect for a father has been a tremendous advantage for Kert, who's had years of hands-on training. "To keep me out of trouble, he'd hand me a pair of snippers and say, 'Here, go cut on that dead bush over there.' I grew up in the business." When it was time to launch his own venture, Kert had a headstart that included both practical experience and loads of referrals.

Even without such a background, yard services offer the flexibility to allow you to specialize in whatever your market and personal capabilities seem to suggest. If you live in a location with an established population of gardeners, you can make extra cash tilling garden plots. If there are numerous small farms in your area, you may want to contract with farmers to cut hay or clear brush. A tree-trimming service can be converted to a firewood business during the slack season, and snow removal can be another income generator in areas with colder climates.

The Franchise Option

Lawn Doctor, Inc., is the 20-year-old brain child of Anthony Giordano, a former New Jersey hardware store owner. He got his start by offering Sunday morning lawn-care clinics for customers who had questions about how to apply chemical fertilizers and weed and bug killers to their lawns. Giordano would listen to their problems, design lawn programs, then sell them the products they needed. Before long, many of his customers were requesting that he actually apply the chemicals to their lawns. It was in working with the equipment available at the time that Giordano saw the need to develop a more reliable system of application.

One day an engineer friend came up with the solution: He claimed he could build a machine that would accurately meter the chemicals directly onto the lawn, based on the amount of ground covered. The best part, and what turned out to be the key to this $25 million success story, was that a degree in agricultural science wouldn't be required to understand the operation of the machine. With some basic training, anyone could do it.

Giordano now has some 300 franchise dealers, most of whom gross between $100,000 and $400,000 annually. The biggest appeal to customers, he says, is that they can get professional lawn care services for just about what it would cost to purchase and apply the products themselves.

Lawn-care franchise fees, which start at about $12,500, are quite modest compared with what you would pay for most other franchises (such as for a retail or fast-food business). The franchise dealer ordinarily isn't required to buy lawn equipment; instead, he leases the necessary equipment from the parent company. At least one franchise company has worked out an arrangement with chemical suppliers so that their dealers can buy in bulk at a discount from vendors in their own areas and pass the savings along to their customers.

Lawn Doctor charges a fee of $22,500, which includes training, advertising and sales support, complete bookkeeping setup and home office guidance for the first year. In return, the company receives a 10 percent royalty plus 5 percent for cooperative advertising from each dealer. "Since we work off the royalties from each dealership, we do everything we can to help the dealer succeed," says Carl Lang. "If we were to leave him on his own, the failure rate would be way up there, which would just waste our time and his money. So he's really hand-nurtured."

Getting the Know-How

"Everybody feels they can cut grass and lay down fertilizer, but it would help to have some kind of horticultural background," advises Bob Early. While a four-year degree in agriculture might be nice, there are faster, cheaper ways of getting the training you need; in fact, much of what you'll need to know can be acquired on the job while you're getting paid. Here are some places to start:

- Horticultural or landscaping courses at your local community college or vocational school can be worthwhile. It would also pay to take a class in small engines — you'll save a lot of money on routine equipment maintenance if you're not totally helpless.

- Your local cooperative extension service, which is usually operated by land grant universities and staffed by knowledgeable people, can be an excellent resource.

- Working part-time or on weekends for an established landscape architect or yard service can be a great way to get started. Your employer can provide you with invaluable hands-on experience in the basics, and later may be able to steer you toward your own clients.

- If you become a franchise dealer, your company will probably provide comprehensive training and field support. Some franchise companies provide toll-free numbers which allow dealers to call and talk to staff agronomists or equipment specialists. In addition, field reps may be assigned to each dealer to provide on-going guidance.

Startup Costs

Equipment and transportation will probably be your biggest investment, but fortunately you won't need an elaborate setup in the beginning. You can start with the basics and, as your business grows, trade up as demand and income permit. Some basic guidelines:

- Buy the best quality equipment you can afford. Good quality mowers, shears, clippers, etc. last longer and make the work easier, and since breakdowns cost you time and money, quality tools are worth the money in the long run.

- It pays to do some comparison shopping when buying equipment. Check *Consumer Reports* or similar guides for product reviews and ask people who have owned and used lawn equipment for recommendations.

- Try to find a good, reliable equipment dealer close to your home. That way, when you need service the amount of "down time" will hopefully be minimized. Does the shop stock an adequate supply of spare parts for your type of equipment? Remember, waiting for ordered parts to come in will cost you money. You might also try to establish a rapport with the shop you do business with. If you have an emergency, its employees might go to the extra effort to really help you out.

- The more sophisticated and automated your equipment, the greater the potential for breakdowns. Simple, straightforward equipment without the frills will be less prone to trouble and easier and less expensive to fix.

The Basics

For ordinary residential lawn work you'll need a 19-inch or 21-inch mower, extra blades, an edger, clippers, and fertilizer spreader. Additional tools will be needed to sharpen and maintain your equipment, and you'll need a few miscellaneous items such as a leaf rake, broom, and trash cans, heavy plastic bags or a tarp for removing debris and clippings. A whipstick or scythe will come in handy for cutting down very tall weeds, and occasionally you'll need an axe, hand saw or small chain saw to cut up downed tree limbs.

As your business grows, you'll want to add a gas-powered hedge trimmer, an electric weed trimmer and a 28- to 30-inch riding mower for larger lawns. Remember that mowers with wider mowing swathes involve a trade-off: although they can speed your work on large lawns, they are necessarily less versatile than smaller mowers. Leaf blowers or lawn vacuums can quickly pay for themselves.

For really vast lawns, brush shredding or hay cutting, you'll need special, heavy-duty equipment: a tractor (about 20 horsepower) with a 60-inch rotary mower for lawns and a sickle bar for cutting hay. You'll need a bush hog for heavily weeded areas or for shredding jobs.

For tree trimming you'll need hand snippers, long-handled loppers, a hand saw and a small chain saw. You'll also need a 14-foot free-standing ladder for trimming the periphery of the tree and some type of harness to secure yourself to the trunk while you work on the large interior branches that require both hands.

Vehicles

As with the other lawn and garden equipment, in the beginning you can get by without a large investment in vehicles. If you're fortunate enough to own a pickup truck, you can easily and cheaply adapt it for use in your business. Kert Sorber converted his pickup to a service truck by adding a good-sized tool box, secured against the back of the cab, and by constructing a wooden frame that extends the sides of the bed to the height of the cab. He lays his 14-foot ladder over the top of the frame to leave the truck bed free for tree limbs and debris.

If you do invest in a truck, consider getting a one-ton pickup, dump truck or flatbed with a hoist underneath the body. Such a vehicle will allow you to haul sod, topsoil or trees and to unload debris easily.

If a truck is out of reach at first, and if your present vehicle has the hauling capacity, you can start with just a trailer. Even if your trailer is to be a temporary mode of hauling, try to get a sturdy one with large tires. If your trailer is too small, it won't hold up to the wear, it can easily be overloaded and won't track well. Even after you've acquired a truck you may need to use your trailer on occasion, so look ahead and buy something of compatible quality. The bed should be no more than eight inches off the ground and the sides should be at least two feet high.

For unloading your pickup or trailer you'll need either a hinged ramp or strong metal or wood planks. You'll also need an assortment of chains, nylon ropes and load binders to secure your equipment.

If you buy into a franchise, vehicles may be part of the package. Lawn Doctor dealers furnish their own trucks, but complete layouts for truck or trailer modifications are provided by the parent company.

Maintenance

Just as important as buying the right equipment is maintaining it properly. Breakdowns can be expensive both in terms of repair costs and time; preventive maintenance can be well worthwhile. Regularly changing your oil and cleaning your filters — especially when there's a lot of blowing dust where you're working — will prolong the life of your equipment. Consider getting a bench grinder so you can do your own blade sharpening, too. Sharp blades make your work easier and make the results more professional-looking.

Safety

Unless you take some safety precautions, it's easy get hurt working with power mowers or cutting tree limbs far above the ground. Here are a few guidelines:

- Dress for the job.

  Many yard care professionals recommend steel-toed, hightop work boots for both summer and winter. Don't ever wear sandals or sneakers when mowing, and heavy trousers are preferable to shorts. Wearing a hat can help guard you against heat exhaustion, and a helmet is a good idea if you're working with others who are cutting tree limbs.

- Remember to drink plenty of fluids when you're working hard. Dehydration makes muscles less efficient and can cause overheating and nausea.

- Wear safety glasses.

  Shatterproof glasses are a good idea when operating rotary edgers and mowers, which can send hidden rocks and glass flying at high speeds. They are essential when operating a chain saw.

- Don't forget ear protection.

  Over a period of time, lawn mowers, tractors and chainsaws can damage your hearing. The headphone-style ear protectors worn by marksmen are preferred by many operators. Plastic earplugs are often uncomfortable. Wax-impregnated cotton gets dirty and builds up moisture in the ear canal, which can lead to infection.

- Never, never use your hand to unclog a stalled mower or snowblower.

    Even with the engine turned off and the clutch released, blades can still turn once they're freed from obstruction — often, fast enough to cause serious injury. It's best to release the clutch, stop the machine and use a trowel or small stick to unclog the blades.

- Know the capabilities of your equipment as well as your own limitations. Don't attempt to use a machine that is too small for the job.

- Use chemicals sparingly and follow directions carefully. Prolonged use of toxic chemicals should be avoided whenever possible.

Other Expenses

One reason that you can start a lawn and garden service with little capital is the fact that you can work from an office in your own home. A home office not only lowers your monthly overhead, but also pays off at tax time, when you can deduct a portion of your rent or mortgage as well as phone and utility bills. You'll need just a few essentials to get started. A telephone — with an answering machine or answering service to take your calls when you're out on the job — is essential, and you'll need a few office supplies including stationery, business cards, invoices and bookkeeping supplies.

Liability insurance is definitely recommended, and you'll probably have to be licensed by your state to dispense chemicals. Licensing requirements vary from state to state, but the Department of Agriculture in your state can direct you to the right office.

What to Charge

Fee-setting is made simple for franchise dealers — usually the parent company determines the fee structure. Lawn Doctor, for example, recommends a $150 per year charge for five visits during the growing season. If you're launching your own independent business, however, setting your fees will take a little homework and some practical experience within your market. For starters, you might simply call a number of other services in your area to find out what their rates are.

In setting your fees, you'll want to take into consideration such variables as the cost and upkeep of your equipment, gas and vehicle expenses, dumping fees, wages for your helpers, insurance, office expenses, and your own time. Some operators charge a flat fee of between $65 and $175 per month. Others, like Kert Sorber, work on an hourly basis. Kert charges $25 an hour for tree trimming, which, he believes, is a fairly competitive rate. "It sounds like a lot of money, but I've got my pace built up to where I can get the job knocked out in just a couple of hours," he says.

Some customers may balk at an hourly rate, so it's a good idea to have an estimate ready just in case. In figuring your estimates, take into account the roughness of the terrain, height of the grass, and the number of trees and shrubs that must be hand trimmed.

You can encourage your customers to talk to their neighbors about your service by offering a neighborhood discount. This not only makes customers happy but also makes your time more productive by cutting travel expenses. It's also wise to establish a minimum fee for jobs outside a two- or three-mile radius.

The Contract Decision

You may decide to require contracts from your customers or opt for service agreements, which can be canceled at any time. One yard service sends customers a new agreement at the end of each year and offers a discount for payment in advance. Whether or not you require a contract, it is always wise to have a signed work order, spelling out exactly what work you'll do and how much you'll be paid *before* you start the job. While most people pay without any problem, if you should have to take a customer to small claims court to collect you'll need a written document on which to base your claim.

Promoting Your Business

More than one lawn-service owner has built a thriving business without investing a cent in advertising, relying instead on word-of-mouth referrals from satisfied customers. But if you'd rather help things along, there are a number of ways you can promote your business without spending a fortune.

- Put a sign on your truck or trailer with your business name and phone number on it.

- Have business cards printed up and give them to anyone who expresses an interest in using your service. Be sure each of your steady customers get a few cards to pass along to friends.

- You can leave your name with local plant nurseries and garden supply stores and post notices on bulletin boards in supermarkets, laundromats and feedstores. To line up commercial accounts, approach local businesses that have large lawns in need of work. You can also check with realtors about vacant homes with yards that need tending.

- Yard services often advertise in the Sunday classified section of their local newspapers. One operator recommends running an ad continuously during the busy season — the rate is lower, and constant exposure brings more consistent results. In addition, paying extra for positioning near the top of the column may be worthwhile.

A Few Helpful Tips

Start out small; if possible, begin your lawn business as a profitable sideline to a steady job that provides a secure income until you are firmly established.

The best way to build a loyal clientele is to develop a reputation for reliability. That means fulfilling your agreements, showing up on time, delivering what you promise.

You can pick up valuable tips and keep abreast of what's happening in the industry as a whole by subscribing to *Lawn Care Industry*. This monthly, tabloid-style trade publication provides news, features on successful businesses, articles on how to improve your business, and ads for new products. (See appendix for ordering information.)

The Professional Lawn Care Association of America offers a number of benefits to members, including "Turf Talks," a newsletter, safety manuals, wage and hour guides, reports on union activity, and a legal update bulletin in which new laws and regulations are reviewed. In addition, members receive reduced rates at national conventions and have the option of buying group medical insurance. The membership fee ranges from $150 to $500, depending on the volume of your business. (See appendix for address.)

A Word About Rewards

As you can see, yard services are strictly for those who don't mind working, but if you're like many successful entrepreneurs, the challenge of hard work is a major attraction. "I don't know, it's crazy," says Kert Sorber. "It's a lot of work but I love to do it." For Sorber and many others, the business offers a satisfying combination of pleasant, physical work and the opportunity to build something on your own. "I work a lot of hours — sometimes it's twelve days a week, thirty-four hours a day — but what's nice about it is you don't have anyone to answer to except yourself and your customer, and if you do a good job, there's a lot of self-satisfaction. You can say, 'Well, I did a good job on this. I'm gonna give myself a raise today.' "

Appendix
Additional Sources of Information

Note: a source for mail-order books, tapes and other materials on self-employment and career change is The New Careers Center, P.O. Box 297, Boulder, CO 80306. Send your name and address for the current catalog/newsletter.

Research and Information Services

The Information Brokers: How to Start and Operate Your Own Fee-Based Service by Kelly Warnken. Ann Arbor: R.R. Bowker Co., 1981.

Information Industry Market Place (annual, at your library.) R.R. Bowker Co.

Child-care Services

Kids Mean Business: How to Turn Your Love of Children Into a Profitable and Wonderfully Satisfying Business, by Barbralu Manning. Boulder: Live Oak, 1985.

Word Processing Services

Word Processing Profits at Home, Peggy Glenn. Aames-Allen, 1983.

How to Create a Successful Word Processing Business by Mimi Will and Nancy Weber. Mountain View, CA: TPW Publishing, 1984.

Catering Services

Freelance Foodcrafting: How to Become Profitably Self-Employed in Your Own Creative Cooking Business by Janet Shown. Boulder, CO: Live Oak, 1983.

Publishing Services

Publishing Newsletters by Howard Hudson. New York: Scribner, 1982.

The Newsletter Editor's Desk Book by Marvin Arth and Helen Ashmore. Parkway Press, 1982.

Image Consulting

Image Consulting: The New Career by Joan Timberlake. Washington, D.C.: Acropolis Books, 1984.

Writing and Editing Services

The Elements of Style by William Strunk, Jr. and E. B. White. New York: MacMillan, 1979.

One Writing Well by William Zinsser. New York: Harper-Row, 1980.

Commonsense Grammer and Style by Robert Morsberger. T.Y. Crowell, 1972.

Household Services

Everything You Need to Know to Start a House Cleaning Service by Mary Pat Johnson. Seattle, WA: Cleaning Consultant Services.

Educational Services

Kids Mean Business by Barbralu Manning. Boulder, CO: Live Oak, 1985.

Lawn and Garden Services

How to Start Your Own Horticulture Business by Laurence Price. Botany Books, 1983.

Lawn Care Industry trade periodical: 7500 Oak Boulevard, Cleveland, OH 44130 (216) 243-8100 ($20/year)

The Professional Lawn Care Association of America, 1225 Johnson Ferry Road NE, Suite B220, Marietta, GA 30067. (404) 977-5222.